MAXnotes®

James Joyce's

A Portrait of the Artist as a Young Man

Text by
Matthew Mitchell
(B.A., Rutgers University)
Department of English
University of Illinois of Urbana-Champaign
Urbana, Illinois

Illustrations by
Thomas E. Cantillon

Research & Education Association

MAXnotes® for
A PORTRAIT OF THE ARTIST AS A YOUNG MAN

Printed in the United States of America

Library of Congress Catalog Card Number 96-67423

International Standard Book Number 0-87891-041-7

MAXnotes® is a registered trademark of
Research & Education Association, Piscataway, New Jersey 08854

What **MAXnotes** *Will Do for You*

This book is intended to help you absorb the essential contents and features of James Joyce's *A Portrait of the Artist as a Young Man* and to help you gain a thorough understanding of the work. The book has been designed to do this more quickly and effectively than any other study guide.

For best results, this **MAXnotes** book should be used as a companion to the actual work, not instead of it. The interaction between the two will greatly benefit you.

To help you in your studies, this book presents the most up-to-date interpretations of every section of the actual work, followed by questions and fully explained answers that will enable you to analyze the material critically. The questions also will help you to test your understanding of the work and will prepare you for discussions and exams.

Meaningful illustrations are included to further enhance your understanding and enjoyment of the literary work. The illustrations are designed to place you into the mood and spirit of the work's settings.

The **MAXnotes** also include summaries, character lists, explanations of plot, and section-by-section analyses. A biography of the author and discussion of the work's historical context will help you put this literary piece into the proper perspective of what is taking place.

The use of this study guide will save you the hours of preparation time that would ordinarily be required to arrive at a complete grasp of this work of literature. You will be well prepared for classroom discussions, homework, and exams. The guidelines that are included for writing papers and reports on various topics will prepare you for any added work which may be assigned.

The **MAXnotes** will take your grades "to the max."

Dr. Max Fogiel
Program Director

Contents

> **Each Chapter includes List of Characters, Summary, Analysis, Study Questions and Answers, and Suggested Essay Topics.**

Introduction

The Life and Work of James Joyce

James Joyce was born in Dublin, Ireland, on February 2, 1882. He was the oldest of ten children, and was born into a comfortable and, by some standards, wealthy home. However, while Joyce was growing up, his family's economic situation became progressively worse.

He was able to attend Clongowes Wood College, an exclusive Jesuit boarding school, from age six to nine, but was forced to leave in 1891 when his father, John Stanislaus Joyce, lost his position as collector of rates in Dublin and could no longer afford to send James to school. After a brief stint at the Christian Brothers' School, James was allowed to attend the Jesuit Belvedere College, thanks to a special arrangement by a former rector at Clongowes, Father John Conmee. Father Conmee had become prefect of studies at Belvedere and, remembering James' ability as a student, arranged for him and his brothers to attend Belvedere without fees.

Joyce was a distinguished student at Belvedere, winning several exhibitions (cash prizes for scholarship in national competitions), and being elected, two years in a row, to the office of prefect of the Sodality of the Blessed Virgin Mary, the highest honor at Belvedere. He became interested in poetry, drama, philosophy and languages, and upon graduation in 1898, entered University College, Dublin at age 16.

Joyce gained a reputation as a radical thinker by reading a paper entitled "Drama and Life" before the Literary and Historical Society. He published an essay in the *Fortnightly Review* entitled "Ibsen's New Drama," defending the controversial playwright. In these and other essays and reviews he wrote during this period, Joyce defended a realistic representation of life on stage, as opposed to what he took to be a sentimental and moralistic nationalism. The trouble he faced getting permission from the president of the university to read "Drama and Life" was the first of many struggles with censorship in Joyce's career. He graduated in 1902, with a degree in modern languages, having studied Italian, French, German, and literary Norwegian as well as Latin.

The Joyce family during this time had been getting both larger and poorer—they had to move around frequently, setting up temporary residences, and were forced to sell many of their possessions to keep creditors at bay. Anxious to escape what he saw as a confining and restrictive environment in Dublin, Joyce left in 1902 to live in self-imposed "exile" in Paris. He had to return, however, in April 1903, as his mother was dying. Mary Jane Joyce died in August of that year, and James Joyce remained in Dublin for over a year, during which time he wrote and published poetry, worked on short stories (some of which were eventually published in the *Dubliners* collection), and began the initial draft of *A Portrait of the Artist as a Young Man*, then entitled *Stephen Hero*.

He left Dublin again in October 1904, with Nora Barnacle. Joyce never returned to Dublin, except for a few brief visits (the last of which was in 1912), though his home city and country continued to dominate his imagination. He lived and taught in Trieste and Rome until World War I, then moved with Nora, their son Giorgio and daughter Lucia to neutral Zurich, where they stayed until 1920. The Joyces then moved to Paris, where they lived until 1940. James and Nora then returned to Zurich, where James Joyce died on January 13, 1941.

A Portrait of the Artist as a Young Man was published in 1916, but the story of its composition covers a ten-year span in Joyce's life. At the end of the novel, we see the words "Dublin 1904—Trieste 1914." This does not mean, as we might expect, that Joyce spent these ten years working on the text as we have it. In 1904, he wrote a combination short story and autobiographical essay entitled "A Portrait of the Artist." When he could not get it published, he began to rewrite it as a novel with the working title *Stephen Hero*. Joyce worked on *Stephen Hero* intermittently for four years, but became ultimately dissatisfied with his lengthy and cumbersome method.

He decided to rewrite the unfinished *Stephen Hero* in five long chapters, selecting and condensing only the most significant episodes in Stephen Dedalus' development. This novel, *A Portrait of the Artist as a Young Man*, was finished in 1914, published serially in *The Egoist* during 1914 and 1915, and finally published by B. W. Huebsch in New York in 1916. As with his other work, Joyce had considerable trouble getting *Portrait* published, both because of the obscenity laws and because of his unconventional literary form.

James Joyce's literary reputation is remarkable when we consider his relatively scant output. Aside from his play, *Exiles*, and a few books of poetry, which have not earned much attention, Joyce's canon consists of a collection of stories, *Dubliners* (1914), and three novels—besides *Portrait*, the mammoth *Ulysses* (1922) and the even more mammoth *Finnegans Wake* (1939). Each of these represents a cornerstone of modernist fiction, and in each work Joyce extends his innovative and experimental style to further limits, leaving a permanent mark on the development of twentieth-century literature. His reputation and influence are as strong today as ever—from high school classrooms to graduate seminars and international professional conferences, Joyce's work continues to generate a staggering degree of critical interest. As Richard Ellmann wrote, "We are still learning to be James Joyce's contemporaries."

Perhaps the first thing that will strike a first-time reader of *A Portrait of the Artist as a Young Man* is the initial strangeness of the language. Joyce's technique is to have the language of the narration try to mirror the linguistic and intellectual development of Stephen Dedalus—therefore, in the first chapter, the vocabulary and sentence structure are more simplistic, limited, and childlike. The narrative is closely aligned with Stephen's consciousness and perspective—therefore, the narrative style could be said to mature along with young Stephen. As the novel progresses, and Stephen becomes better acclimatized to his world, the language expands and develops accordingly.

Whereas in the *Stephen Hero* stage of the novel's composition Joyce was trying to cram every detail about Stephen's life into the narrative, in *A Portrait of the Artist as a Young Man* he exercises much more selectivity. The novel presents only the most important events in Stephen's life, without as much attention to chronological and temporal sequence as we would find in a traditional novel. The subject of the novel is Stephen's internal intellectual and artistic development, so the conflicts and climaxes which would motivate a traditionally plotted novel are in this case a matter of internal relations. A conflict is important because it is so for Stephen; a climax is such because of its importance in Stephen's ultimate spiritual development Each scene or episode in the novel, then, will be loaded with significance on a number of levels.

Fundamental to the technique and structure of this novel is Joyce's conception of *epiphany.* An epiphany, as Joyce conceives it, is a moment of intense perception, or a feeling of total understanding; one's life is punctuated by such moments. In *Stephen Hero,* Joyce defines his (and Stephen's) conception of epiphany thus:

> By an epiphany he meant a sudden spiritual manifestation, whether in the vulgarity of speech or of gesture or in a memorable phase of the mind itself. He believed that it was for the man of letters to record these epiphanies with extreme care, seeing that they themselves are the most delicate and evanescent of moments.

The epiphany is a moment of extreme significance for the subject, or the beholder, and for the object which he or she observes—the epiphany reveals something essential about the person or thing that is observed. Stephen and Joyce understand that the purpose of the artist is to record and present these moments of privileged spiritual insight. The religious source of Joyce's conception (the feast day celebrating the revelation of the infant Christ to the Magi) indicates that this is a spiritual, non-rational conception of knowledge.

A Portrait of the Artist as a Young Man represents the growth and development of Stephen's soul, and the novel is structured around the epiphanies Stephen experiences while growing up. Thus, the narrator is less concerned with dates, ages, time, and a clear chronological sequence. Joyce's conception of epiphany allows us to view time in the novel as a coalescence of past, present, and future. This means, then, for our reading and interpretation of the novel, that each scene will be dense with significance, shedding light on past events in the narrative as well as looking forward to future developments. Joyce is extremely selective—there are many gaps in the story of Stephen's life we must fill in while reading. But this means that we must pay extra attention to the episodes we are given, and the language in which they are told.

Historical Background

A Portrait of the Artist as a Young Man is an autobiographical novel—Stephen Dedalus is Joyce's fictional figure for himself in the early years of his life, and the events in the novel closely parallel those of Joyce's own life. We should be careful not to push this identification of Stephen with young Joyce too far, for the author of a novel is certainly free to take creative liberties that the author of a strict biography would not take. The novel should and does stand as an autonomous artifact in its own right. It is clear, however, that the historical and cultural context of Dublin in the 1890s is as crucial toward our understanding of Stephen Dedalus and his world as it is toward our understanding of Joyce and his world.

Though the novel is ambiguous when it comes to precise dates, the events in *A Portrait of the Artist as a Young Man* cover the period from roughly 1890 through the end of the century. Ireland was then, as it indeed is now, a country torn apart by politics and religion. The Republic of Ireland had not yet won its independence from the British crown, though the liberation movement was fervent. Battle lines were drawn between Protestants and Catholics. Institutionalized religious discrimination had long been used by the Protestant British government as a means of division and control of the Irish-Catholic population, and this naturally trickled down into day-to-day hostility and resentment between Protestant and Catholic people in Ireland. The lines were not always quite this clear, however; there were many among the liberationists who criticized the Catholic church for hindering the anti-British cause.

This anti-Catholic sentiment—which we hear voiced in the novel by Stephen's father and Mr. Casey at Christmas dinner in Chapter 1—is due in large degree to the downfall of Charles Stewart Parnell. Parnell was a liberation leader who was extremely popular, powerful and influential; he was seen by many as the savior of Ireland. However, a scandal erupted in 1889 and 1890, when Captain William Henry O'Shea filed for divorce from his wife, Kitty, on grounds of her adultery with Parnell. The controversy surrounding this affair led directly to the dissolution of Parnell's party, and he died within a year. Parnell's devotees then saw him as a kind of tragic hero, and criticized the Catholic church for their role in condemning the Irish Nationalist leader. They would argue that Parnell's "sin" was a personal matter that should not have jeopardized what they saw as their greatest hope for independence. Joyce, in particular, saw Parnell's case as an apt illustration of what was wrong with Ireland: he was persecuted and discredited, on moralistic grounds, by the same people he had spent his life trying to liberate.

As the largest and most cosmopolitan city in Ireland, Dublin was a hotbed of political and religious conflict in the 1890s. In the arts, too, there was fierce debate as to what direction Ireland should take. The poet and playwright William Butler Yeats was instrumental in working toward an Irish literature, in English, that could become a recognized and appreciated part of European culture. At the same time, however, a more conservative nationalist element called for, along with a renewed interest in Irish folklore and a Gaelic language, positive or "pure" representations of Irish culture in the arts. Therefore, much of the groundbreaking dramatic work of Yeats and J. M. Synge was condemned loudly by many critics, reviewers, and audiences. Joyce associated this kind of attitude with a puritanical orthodoxy which he dislikes intensely. His personal literary development tended to move apart from the Irish literary revival.

It stands to reason, then, that Joyce would feel a need to "escape" from Ireland. He was more interested in studying Italian or German than Gaelic, and was more interested in reading European literature than Irish folktales. However, it is equally clear that the end of the nineteenth century in Dublin, and the political and cultural conflicts which dominated the world into which Joyce grew, continued to have a profound grip on his imagination. Dublin is the setting for all of his literary work, even though he was living in Europe while most of it was written. These formative years, which are detailed in *A Portrait of the Artist as a Young Man,* are the only time Joyce really lived in Ireland. His self-imposed "exile," however, should not be seen as a total rejection of Ireland. He retained a profoundly ambivalent attitude toward his home city for the rest of his life; he despised aspects of it, but remained fascinated by it.

The publication of Joyce's work caused something of a scandal in Dublin. His portrayal of the city is not always flattering, and he frequently incorporates real people from the city into his work. It is obvious why a nationalistic reader, who thinks that Irish literature should be primarily concerned with representing Ireland in a positive light, would think Joyce something of a national embarrassment. Initial reviews a *A Portrait of the Artist as a Young Man*, both in Ireland and abroad, often alternated between recognition and praise of the artistic skill of the novel, while balking at some of the offensive and crude realism in the novel.

For a first novel, Joyce's *Portrait* got a substantial critical response, gaining the attention of contemporary literary figures such as Ezra Pound, W. B. Yeats, H. G. Wells, and Wyndham Lewis. He did not gain his full reputation as an avant-garde innovator in the art of prose, however, until the publication of *Ulysses*, which is more radical in its formal departures from literary conventions.

A Portrait of the Artist as a Young Man will obviously have a strong appeal to young adults with a Catholic upbringing or an artistic disposition. Such students will surely identify specifically with much of Stephen's experience. However, the more general theme of a young person coming of age, and the complex interplay of rebellion and conformity which this involves—growing away from the world of parents and the church as well as growing within it—has had and will continue to have a more universal appeal to younger readers from various backgrounds.

Master List of Characters

Simon Dedalus—*Stephen's father, originally from the city of Cork, a friendly and humorous man, a strong and vocal supporter of Parnell; his wealth declines throughout the novel.*

Mary Dedalus—*Stephen's mother, a quiet, religious woman, who wants Stephen to observe his Easter duties at the end of the novel.*

Stephen Dedalus—*The protagonist and focal character of the narrative; it is essentially "his" story we are reading, following him from about age six until age eighteen, as he grows through and past the Catholic church, deciding finally to leave Dublin for Europe to become an artist.*

Uncle Charles—*Simon's uncle, Stephen's granduncle, who lives with the Dedalus family in the early stage of the novel; trying to preserve calm with Mrs. Dedalus, he remains noncommittal through the Christmas dinner argument.*

Dante—*Stephen's governess, a nickname for "aunt." A well-read and intelligent woman who teaches Stephen geography. She is vehement in her devotion to the Catholic church, and joins it in condemning Parnell despite her desire for liberation.*

Brigid—*The Dedalus' maid; she only appears in the first chapter, and stands as an indication of their relative wealth as the novel begins.*

Mr. Casey—*A close friend of the Dedalus family, who attends Christmas dinner, and is instrumental in provoking the argument with Dante. Mr. Casey, like Mr. Dedalus, is a devout supporter of Parnell.*

Rody Kickham—*A student at Clongowes, a good football player and, according to young Stephen, a "descent fellow."*

Nasty Roche—*A student at Clongowes, whose father is a magistrate. He questions Stephen about his own father, and teases him about his unusual name. Stephen considers him a "stink."*

Wells—*The student at Clongowes who pushes Stephen into the square ditch (the drainage for the outhouse). He teases and intimidates Stephen, but when it is clear that he has made Stephen ill by pushing him into the ditch, Wells begs him not to tell the rector.*

Jack Lawton—*Classmate of Stephen's at Clongowes; he is Stephen's "rival" in academic classroom competitions.*

Simon Moonan and Tusker Boyle—*Students at Clongowes, in Stephen's class, who were allegedly caught "smugging" (a mild form of homosexual petting) with three older students. Stephen and the others discuss how Moonan and Boyle will be flogged.*

Father Arnall—*Stephen's math and Latin teacher at Clongowes; he excuses Stephen from his lesson since he broke his glasses. He reappears in Chapter Three, and leads the retreat of St. Francis Xavier.*

Fleming—*A student at Clongowes, who is friendly and sympathetic to Stephen. He asks if Stephen is okay when he wakes up ill, then urges him to stay in bed.*

Father Dolan—*The prefect of studies and disciplinarian at Clongowes, who comes in and interrupts Latin class.*

Brother Michael—*The medical attendant at the infirmary when Stephen is ill.*

Athy—*The older student (in the third of grammar) who Stephen meets in the infirmary. He is friendly and tells Stephen riddles.*

Eileen—*A friend of Stephen's at home. She is a Protestant, and Stephen associates her white hands with the tower of Ivory.*

Cecil Thunder—*A classmate of Stephen's at Clongowes.*

Corrigan—*One of the older students involved in the smuggling incident with Moonan and Boyle; given the choice between expulsion and flogging, Athy claims that Corrigan opted for flogging by Mr. Gleeson.*

Mr. Harford—*Stephen's writing teacher at Clongowes.*

Father Conmee—*The rector at Clongowes; Stephen goes to speak to him about Father Dolan; Father Conmee is sympathetic and promises to speak to the prefect.*

Mike Flynn—*An old friend of Simon Dedalus, who is Stephen's running trainer.*

Aubrey Mills—*Stephen's childhood friend at home after Stephen leaves Clongowes; the two boys play adventure games together.*

Maurice—*Stephen's younger brother, who is sent with Stephen to Belvedere College.*

Vincent Heron—*Stephen's friend, antagonist, and "rival" at Belvedere; he delights in Stephen's acts of "heresy," yet condemns Byron, Stephen's favorite poet, as a heretic.*

Wallis—*Heron's sidekick; Stephen sees them together smoking outside of the play, and they, jokingly, make him recite the* Confiteor.

Mr. Tate—*Stephen's English teacher at Belvedere, who accuses Stephen of heresy in an essay.*

Boland and Nash—*Heron's two friends; the "dunce" and "idler" of the class, respectively. They try to argue with Stephen about poetry, mostly aping Heron's opinion that Tennyson is the "best poet." They condemn Stephen's favorite, Byron, as a heretic.*

Doyle—*The director of the play Stephen is in at Belvedere.*

Johnny Cashman—*An old man to whom Stephen and his father speak while visiting Cork; Johnny claims to know many of Stephen's ancestors.*

E--- C--- / Emma—*The girl to whom Stephen addresses his poems; she doesn't actually appear in the novel, except through Stephen's memories (the "her" throughout Chapter 5).*

Ennis—*A classmate of Stephen's at Belvedere.*

Old Woman—*Stephen meets her in the street. She directs him to the Church Street chapel.*

Priest—*The priest at the Church Street chapel to whom Stephen confesses, rather than the priest at the retreat.*

The Director—*At Belvedere College, he asks Stephen if he has considered joining the priesthood.*

Dan Crosby—*A tutor; goes with Simon Dedalus to find out about the university for Stephen.*

Dwyer, Towser, Shuley, Ennis, Connolly—*Acquaintances of Stephen; he sees them swimming as he walks along the strand. They seem to him grotesque and immature.*

Katey, Boody, Maggie—*Stephen's younger sisters.*

Cranly—*Stephen's friend and confidant at the university; Stephen speaks to him about his plans to leave Ireland, and Cranly urges Stephen to appease him mother and observe his Easter duties.*

Davin—*A friend of Stephen's at the university; he is from a rural area of Ireland, a "peasant student," the other students tend to romanticize his accent and his "simple" ways.*

Dean of Studies—*An Englishman who talks with Stephen about his developing theory of aesthetics.*

Moynihan—*A fellow university student who tells ribald jokes during lecture.*

Professor of Physics—*Stephen attends his lecture, but is not engaged.*

MacAlister—*A fellow student from the north of Ireland whom Stephen dislikes intensely.*

MacCann—*A student at the university, a socialist and political activist who engages Stephen in a brief public debate outside of the physics lecture.*

Temple—*A student at the university, a gypsy and a socialist, he admires Stephen immensely, much to the chagrin of Cranly, who finds Temple repulsive.*

Lynch—*A student at the university, to whom Stephen talks about his theory of aesthetics and morality.*

Donovan—*A student who Stephen and Lynch encounter during their walk; Stephen dislikes him.*

Father Moran—*A priest with whom Stephen thinks Emma has been flirting.*

Dixon—*The medical student at the library with Cranly.*

The Captain—*A dwarfish old man who Stephen, Dixon, and Cranly see at the library.*

O'Keefe—*A student who riles Temple outside the library.*

Goggins—*A stout student, part of the crowd outside the library.*

Glynn—*A young man at the library.*

Summary of the Novel

A Portrait of the Artist as a Young Man covers the childhood and adolescence of Stephen Dedalus. We see him, over the course of the novel, grow from a little boy to a young man of eighteen who has decided to leave his country for Europe, in order to be an artist.

At the start of the novel, Stephen is a young boy, probably about five-years-old. He is one of the younger students at Clongowes Wood College for boys (a Jesuit elementary school, not a "college" in the American sense). He had been pushed into an outhouse drainage ditch by a student named Wells a few days earlier, and he wakes up ill. While in the infirmary, Stephen dreams of going home for the Christmas holidays. We then see the Dedalus family at Christmas dinner, and a heated argument erupts between Stephen's father and Dante, Stephen's governess, about Parnell and the Catholic church. Back at school, Stephen has broken his glasses and has been excused from classwork by his teacher, Father Arnall. The prefect of studies, Father Dolan, comes into class to discipline the students, and singles out Stephen as a "lazy idle little loafer." Stephen is pandied (his knuckles beaten with a bat) in front of the class, and feels the injustice of his punishment deeply. The other students urge him to speak to the rector of the college. He gets up the courage to do so, and the rector promises to speak to Father Dolan. Stephen is cheered by the other students.

In the second chapter, Stephen is a few years older. He is no longer at Clongowes but at Belvedere College. He has started to become interested in literature, and tends to romanticize his life based on what he reads. He tries to write a poem to the girl he loves, but cannot. He is in a play at Belvedere, and outside of the theater he sees two other students, Heron and Wallis, who tease him about the play, and jokingly make him recite the *Confiteor*. Stephen, while doing so, remembers a recent incident when his English teacher suspected him of heresy. Stephen takes a trip to Cork with his father, and his father shows him the town where he was born and raised, and the school he attended when he was Stephen's age. Back in Dublin, Stephen wins a sum of money for an essay competition, and, for a brief time, treats himself and his family to a "season of pleasure." When the money runs out, we can see him wandering the red light districts of Dublin, fantasizing about the prostitutes. As the chapter ends, Stephen has his first experience with a prostitute.

In Chapter Three, it is apparent that Stephen has made a habit of soliciting prostitutes. He goes through the motions in school and at church, and is not bothered by the duplicity of his life. He goes on a religious retreat with his class, and the priest's sermon about sin and damnation affects Stephen deeply. He repents, goes to confession at the chapel across town, and takes communion.

Stephen has now dedicated his life to God. He prays constantly, and goes about mortifying his senses. He has completely renounced his sinful relations with the prostitutes, and the director at Belvedere speaks to him about becoming a priest. The idea first seems to appeal to Stephen, but he ultimately decides that he could not become a priest.

His father is making plans for Stephen, now 16, to enter the university. Walking along the seashore one afternoon, thinking about poetry, Stephen sees a young woman bathing. They stare at each other, but do not speak. Stephen takes this as a spiritual sign, and he excitedly decides to dedicate his life to art.

In the final chapter, Stephen is at the university. He is lazy about his classes but vehement about his developing theory of aesthetics. He refuses to sign a political petition, trying to set himself apart from the concerns of his country's politics or religion. Talking to his close friend, Cranly, Stephen announces that he has decided to leave Ireland for Europe to pursue his artistic vocation. The novel closes with a few pages out of Stephen's diary, as he makes plans to leave for the continent.

Estimated Reading Time

A Portrait of the Artist as a Young Man is broken up into five chapters—the first four are about equal in length; the fifth is about twice as long as the others. Each chapter should take about an hour to read, though the language and unconventional narration style may take some getting used to. Spending two separate hour-long sittings on the fifth chapter, a student should be able to read the novel in six one-hour sittings.

Chapter 1

New Characters:

Mr. Dedalus: *Stephen's father*

Mrs. Dedalus: *Stephen's mother*

Stephen Dedalus: *the protagonist and focal character of the narrative*

Uncle Charles: *Stephen's granduncle*

Dante: *Stephen's governess*

Brigid: *the Dedalus' maid*

Rody Kickham: *student at Clongowes*

Nasty Roche: *student at Clongowes*

Wells: *student at Clongowes who pushed Stephen into the ditch*

Simon Moonan: *student at Clongowes, caught "smugging"*

Tusker Boyle: *student at Clongowes, caught "smugging" with Simon*

Jack Lawton: *Stephen's competitor in class*

Father Arnall: *Stephen's math and Latin teacher*

Fleming: *student at Clongowes; Stephen's friend*

Father Dolan: *prefect of studies at Clongowes*

Brother Michael: *medical attendant in the infirmary*

Athy: *student at Clongowes*

Mr. Casey: *friend of the Dedalus family*

Eileen: *Stephen's friend, a Protestant*

Cecil Thunder: *student at Clongowes*

Corrigan: *older student at Clongowes*

Mr. Gleeson: *teacher at Clongowes, will flog Corrigan*

Mr. Harford: *Stephen's writing teacher at Clongowes*

Father Conmee: *the rector at Clongowes*

Summary

In the first brief section of the chapter, Stephen is very young. He remembers a story his father told him, and a song he likes to sing. He thinks about Dante, and her brushes (maroon for Michael Davitt, green for Parnell—both Irish nationalist leaders), and about their neighbors, the Vances.

Next, Stephen is at Clongowes Wood College. Stephen is playing football (soccer) with the others, but stays outside of the action because he is younger, smaller, and weaker. He remembers another student, Nasty Roche, questioning him about his name and his father. He remembers being left at school by his mother and father, his mother crying, and his father telling him to write if he wanted anything, and "never to peach on a fellow." He remembers being pushed into a drainage ditch by a student named Wells. Stephen is cold and obviously homesick, and is counting the days until Christmas break.

The boys go inside, into a math class. The teacher, Father Arnall, has a game where the students are divided into teams, York and Lancaster (after the English War of the Roses), and Stephen is struggling with the difficult math. He and another student, Jack Lawton, are constantly competing for first place in these classroom games.

At dinner, Stephen is not hungry and only drinks tea. He feels ill, and thinks about being home. Later, in the playroom, he is teased by Wells about whether or not he kisses his mother before going to bed. In study hall, he changes the number on his desk from 27 to 26 days until the Christmas holiday. He tries to study geography but cannot concentrate. His mind wanders, and he thinks about his father, Dante, and Mr. Casey arguing about politics—Stephen does not understand politics, but wishes he did.

They go to chapel for night prayers, and then go to be. In bed, Stephen fantasizes about traveling home for the holidays. When he wakes up, he feels even more ill, and his friend Fleming tells him to stay in bed. Wells, worried that he has made Stephen ill by pushing him into the ditch, begs Stephen not to tell on him. The prefect comes, and, convinced that Stephen is really ill, tells him to go to the infirmary. In the infirmary, Stephen meets Brother Michael, and thinks once again of home and his parents. He is afraid he might die before he sees them again. He talks to an older boy, Athy, who tells him riddles. In the infirmary, Stephen thinks about his father and his grandfather, and about the death of Parnell.

In the next section, Stephen is home for Christmas dinner. His family, Dante, and Mr. Casey are there. The meal is lavish, prepared and served by servants. An argument erupts at the table between Mr. Dedalus, Mr. Casey, and Dante about the Catholic church and its role in political matters. Stephen's mother and Uncle Charles try to end it, not taking sides and pleading that they not discuss politics at Christmas. The discussion continues, and moves to the more specific and recent issue of Parnell and the role of the church in his downfall. Despite the urgings of Mrs. Dedalus and Uncle Charles, the conflict continues on a subtler level, as Mr. Casey tells an "instructive" anecdote aimed to provoke Dante, about spitting in the eye of a woman who was taunting him about Parnell. This brings the conflict to a boil, and the section ends with Mr. Casey and Dante shouting at each other across the table, Mr. Casey saying "no God for Ireland," and Dante calling him a blasphemer. As Dante storms out of the room, Stephen notices that Mr. Casey and his father are crying for Parnell.

In the next section, Stephen is back at Clongowes. He and the other students are talking about some boys who were in trouble at the school—some say they stole cash, others that they drank the altar wine, and Athy says they are all wrong, that the boys were caught "smugging," a mild form of homosexual petting. The conversation then moves to the question of what punishment the boys will receive. The younger of the five, Simon Moonan and Tusker Boyle, will be flogged, while the three older boys can choose between expulsion and flogging.

They are called in from the playground, and in writing class Stephen has trouble because he has broken his glasses on the

cinderpath. In Latin class, Father Arnall has exempted Stephen from work. The prefect of studies comes in to intimidate and discipline the students. First, he punishes Fleming, who Father Arnall had made kneel in the aisle for writing a bad theme and missing a question in grammar. He then singles out Stephen, and punishes him for not working, thinking that Stephen has tricked Father Arnall. When he is gone, Father Arnall lets them return to their seats, and Stephen is bewildered and upset at his unfair punishment.

Outside of the class, the other boys sympathize with Stephen, and urge him to go tell the rector. At lunch, Stephen decides that he will go and speak to the rector, though he remains hesitant and unsure until the last minute. As he leaves the refectory, he gets up the courage to turn and climb the stairs to the rector's office.

After Stephen explains his case, the rector says that he is sure that Father Dolan made a mistake, and that he will speak to him. Stephen hurries out to the other students, who loudly cheer his success, lifting him onto their shoulders. The crowd dissipates, and at the end of the chapter Stephen is standing alone as the other students play cricket.

Analysis

The novel begins with a cliched storytelling device: "Once upon a time...," be we soon learn that this is not a conventional narrative. The initially confusing and opaque first paragraph represents a story Mr. Dedalus had told Stephen, who is very young in this first short section of the novel. Stephen is identified with the subject of the story ("He was baby tuckoo"), and it quickly becomes clear that the narrative is closely aligned with his perspective. The narrative is thus purposely limited by his immature vocabulary. For example, when we read, "his father looked at him through a glass: he had a hair face," we are to understand that Stephen does not yet know the word "beard." Stephen remembers a song he likes to sing, "O, the wild rose blossoms / On the little green place," but the narrator shows us that he is not yet old enough to pronounce it correctly: "O, the green wothe botheth." These first two pages are fragmentary and scattered, in order to represent the associative and impression-istic mind of a young child. Even in these seemingly random and

incoherent fragments of his consciousness, the greater themes of the novel and the motivating forces of Stephen's world are represented in microcosm. The political world is represented by Dante's two brushes. The world of his family is shown to us. Sexuality is hinted at: ("when he was grown up he was going to marry Eileen"). Art is represented through his father's story and Stephen's song.

In these early pages of the novel, we are being introduced to the world of the protagonist, Stephen Dedalus, as well as being shown Joyce's original and unusual narrative style. Although it is not a first-person narrative, the narrator is intimately engaged with Stephen's consciousness throughout. This method has been called "free indirect discourse," a third-person narrator, with many first-person characteristics. The narrator does not have a voice that is clearly distinct from Stephen's, and he does not comment explicitly on the action. It is not a detached or conventionally omniscient storyteller, but is rather closely aligned with Stephen's consciousness, mirroring his intellectual and linguistic development. It is not clear that the narrator knows more than Stephen does. Can the narrator, then, like the young man, be mistaken or deluded? Throughout the novel, there is the persistent possibility that we should not take the narrator's words at face value, and that Stephen is being treated by the author with a subtle irony.

Throughout the first chapter, Joyce is trying to recreate the impressionistic world of a young child. After the first brief section, Stephen is older—probably about five or six years old. The novel is not always clear about dates, ages, and chronological time. Months and years will pass without mention, and we must infer Stephen's age and maturity from various clues in the narration. A person's life, as Joyce conceives it, is not significant because of its events or the order and circumstances in which they occur. Rather, memories are always colored by the present moment and expectations for the future; likewise, the present is always colored by memories and past experiences. Joyce's narrative tries to capture this more fluid conception of the protagonist's life, and is thus not concerned with establishing clear dates and times.

The narrative in the first chapter is highly impressionistic. Stephen's senses are active—sight, smell, sound, and touch are all emphasized throughout. He is sensitive to color, and especially to hot and cold. His experience of being at school at Clongowes is

characteristically cold and damp; his memories of home are characteristically warm and dry. This betrays both a childlike sensitivity to simple sense perception, as well as suggesting the early stages of Stephen's developing artistic disposition. Stephen's young imagination is especially vivid, and his sense perceptions are often, in this chapter, closely associated with an imaginative flight (such as when he dreams of going home).

Stephen's reactions to his world are colored heavily by the influence of others—Dante, his father, and the older students. When Wells is questioning Stephen about whether or not he kisses his mother before going to bed, and then teases him when he says yes and when he says no, Stephen despairs: "What was the right answer to the question? He had given two and still Wells laughed." It is not that Stephen is concerned with the true answer, but with the *right* one, the one that will allow him to fit into the social situation at hand. Stephen is, throughout the first chapter, trying to acclimatize himself to the existing social, political, and familial structures of his world. He is younger and smaller than the other students, and not at all self-confident.

Another aspect of the older students' influence on young Stephen is his tendency to use their slang to explain things. When Stephen encounters some strange and ambiguous graffiti in the square, he confidently asserts, "Some fellows had drawn it there for a cod." He is using his classmates' slang, but it is not clear that he is at home with their language, that he either understands the joke itself, or even what a "cod" is at all. The words seem somewhat uncomfortable to him, as if he is quoting someone else. He will use this, throughout the chapter, as a way of "understanding" what is going on around him, but it is as if we don't quite believe that he does in fact understand.

It is important to recognize that Stephen's way of making sense involves a particular specific concern with language, here in the first chapter as throughout the novel. He is fascinated by words as names—his own name, as well as others:

> God was God's name just as his name was Stephen. *Dieu* was the French for God and that was God's name too; and when anyone prayed to God and said *Dieu* then God knew at once that it was a French person that was praying.

This passage represents an interesting and illustrative combination of Stephen's early capacity for abstract, complex, metaphysical thought, as well as the comically childlike simplicity of his understanding of language and religion. Stephen is fascinated by language, by the very fact that a word can represent a person, or even God.

Stephen is also intrigued by meaning, especially cases of double meaning: "He kept his hands in the sidepockets of his belted grey suit. That was a belt round his pocket. And belt was also to give a fellow a belt." Note the confident simplicity of Stephen's tone. Recognizing a new aspect of language is, for Stephen, to have gained a new level of understanding.

Stephen's life at Clongowes is presented as alternating between a hostile and unpleasant present and a more desirable alternative. The strength of his young imagination contributes greatly to this— he is constantly imagining, in vivid detail, his impending journey home for the holidays. While his impression of Clongowes is constantly couched in terms of coldness and wetness, unfriend-liness and unfamiliarity, he imagines his home as warm, dry, familiar, and friendly. So it is appropriate that the next section, as Stephen is home at Christmas, begins with this description:

> A great fire, banked high and red, flamed in the grate and under the ivytwined branches of the chandelier the Christmas table was spread.

The narrator, assuming Stephen's level of associations, sets up the scene at home using language of warmth, comfort, and tranquility. Stephen is more at ease there, though he is still an outsider. This is the first year he is old enough to sit with the adults, so he feels a distance and alienation from them similar to what he felt at Clongowes. He is a total stranger to the world of politics that dominates their discussion, and once again we see him sit silently, observing and reacting rather than acting and speaking himself.

Stephen's understanding of politics, as described in the earlier section, is typical in its binary construction:

> He wondered if they were arguing at home about that. That was called politics. There were two sides in it: Dante was on

one side and his father and Mr. Casey were on the other side but his mother and Uncle Charles were on no side. Every day there was something in the paper about it. It pained him that he did not know well what politics meant...

The world which Stephen is growing into is highly politically charged—he is aware of this, but also aware that he does not understand it and must remain, for the time being, outside of this dynamic.

The argument at Christmas dinner both confirms and alters the conception of politics Stephen had. The "two sides," at his house anyway, are clear. Mr. Casey and his father are devout supporters of Parnell, and spare no words in their criticism and even condemnation of the Catholic church. Dante, though also a supporter of Irish liberation, is foremost a Catholic, and condemns Parnell for his adulterous affair. We hear Stephen remember her ripping the green velvet back from the Parnell brush when the scandal broke.

Stephen is, of course, silent during the argument, though Uncle Charles and Dante periodically refer to his presence, scolding Mr. Dedalus for his language in front of the child. Although he is silent and passive, we are aware that his mind, as ever, is active. As he tries to understand the conflict he has witnessed, he must complicate some of the categories and binaries he has constructed:

> Stephen looked with affection at Mr. Casey's face which stared across the table over his joined hands.... But why was he against the priests? Because Dante must be right then. But he had heard his father say that she was a spoiled nun and that she had come out of the convent in the Alleghanies when her brother had got the money from the savages for the trinkets and the chainies. Perhaps that made her severe against Parnell.

Stephen clearly does not understand the terms of the conflict, and in a sense the specifics are not what are important here. This is a significant, perhaps epiphanous, moment in Stephen's life—not because of what he learned about Irish politics at the dinner table, but because he is forced to consider his sources of authority. He likes his father, Dante and Mr. Casey equally, and must come to terms with their radical disagreement. This memory becomes significant for Stephen because of its more general implications for his understanding of national and religious politics, which he eventually seeks to escape altogether. The stable world of Stephen's binaries—right, wrong; good, bad—seems threatened here.

Mr. Dedalus' vocal and quite crass questioning of Catholic authority shocks Stephen, but influences him profoundly. His father's criticism of the church prefigures his own questioning of Jesuit authority at the end of this chapter, and ultimately his rejection of the church as a young adult.

If we understand Stephen as a figure for the young artist, then we can see Clongowes and the Jesuit authority as representing many of the forces active in Ireland that, in Joyce's conception, repressed the artist. First, the incident with Wells pushing him into the ditch places Stephen in the role of the righteous innocent victim, which the other boys seem to support by agreeing that "it was a mean thing to do." He comes to embrace this image as the novel progresses. His alienation from the other students and his existence along the margins of the social scene at the school prefigure his sense of the necessity of "exile" from his home country.

When Stephen, at the start of the final section of this chapter, hears the other students discussing Simon Moonan and Tusker Boyle, he is primarily trying to figure out what they did wrong; he does not think to question that they did wrong. It would never occur to him to question the school authorities here. It is clear that Stephen is convinced that the students must have been doing something wrong for them to be punished so severely.

When he is punished unjustly by Father Dolan, he seems immediately certain that the authority, in this case, has made a mistake. Stephen never wavers in his moral indignation—he is certain that the punishment was indeed "cruel and unfair." The pain of his punishment is moral rather than physical—his ego and his integrity are hurt more than his hand. Likewise, his hesitation when it comes to informing the rector is practical, not moral—he thinks the rector might not believe him, in which case the other students will laugh at him. That might just mean more pandying at the hands of Father Dolan. However, for the first time in the novel, Stephen decides to act of his own accord, and his certainty is rewarded. His "success" in going to speak to the rector is one of many "climaxes" in the novel. It represents an important moment in the development of Stephen's soul; this questioning of author-ity prefigures his later rebellions.

At the end of the chapter, the tone is triumphant. Stephen is cheered by his classmates, and carried on their shoulders—symbolically centralized among them, rather than marginalized. However, the crowd soon dissipates and Stephen is alone once again. He observes rather than participates in the cricket match, but this time his isolation and distance seem different. Rather than feeling uncomfortably alienated, he feels good to be alone—"He was happy and free." This kind of "happy exile," or willful alienation, will come to characterize Stephen's relationship with the politics and religion of his country as he gets older. He is still outside of the game as the chapter ends, but he has achieved an apparently significant moral victory for himself.

Study Questions

1. Through which characters' consciousness is the narrative focused?

2. Who is "baby tuckoo"?

3. What is the significance of Dante's maroon and green brushes?

4. What advice does Stephen's father give him as they leave him off at Clongowes?

5. Why did Wells push Stephen into the ditch?

6. How does Mrs. Dedalus respond to the argument at the Christmas dinner table?

7. What is the story Mr. Casey tells at dinner?

8. According to Athy, why are Simon Moonan and Tusker Boyle in trouble?

9. Why was Stephen exempt from classwork by Father Arnall?

10. What do Stephen's classmates encourage him to do after Father Conmee pandies him?

Answers

1. The narrative is focused, in the style of "free indirect discourse," through Stephen Dedalus' consciousness.

2. "Baby Tuckoo" is the "nicens little boy" in the story Stephen's father tells him when he is very young. It is a figure for Stephen himself.

3. The maroon brush stands for Michael Davitt, and the green brush stands for Parnell, the famous Irish nationalist leaders.

4. He tells him to write home if he wanted anything, and "whatever he did, never to peach on a fellow."

5. Wells pushed Stephen into the ditch because Stephen refused to swap his snuffbox for Wells' "seasoned hacking chestnut."

6. Mrs. Dedalus does not take sides in the debate. She wants them to refrain from discussing politics, if only on this one day of the year, Christmas.

7. Mr. Casey tells a story, designed to provoke Dante, about being harassed by a woman who was condemning Parnell's affair with Kitty O'Shea. He says that he heard her call Kitty O'Shea a name that he won't repeat, and so he spit his mouthful of tobacco juice in her face.

8. He says that they were caught in the square with three older students "smugging." Since homosexual activity is against the rules at Clongowes, they are to be flogged.

9. Stephen was exempted from classwork until his new glasses arrive; he accidentally broke them when he fell on the cinderpath, and cannot see well enough without them to participate.

10. Stephen's classmates urge him to go speak to the rector, since his punishment was cruel and unfair.

Suggested Essay Topics

1. Discuss Stephen's relationship with language in his chapter. Why is his interest in language significant at this early age? Does this make him more or less engaged with the other students his age? Are there any political implications, in light of the Irish nationalist movement, to his identification of English as "his" language?

2. At various points in this chapter, Stephen proposes a theory of language based upon onomatopoeia—the idea that a word's sound has a kind of concordance to its meaning. Examples of onamatopoeia would be "splat, bam, pow." In what ways does Joyce's narration in this chapter use the *sound* of language to achieve its effects? How would you characterize the tone of the narrator at the start of the chapter? At the end? Is there a thematic connection?

3. Stephen's senses are very acute, and throughout the first chapter Joyce makes us aware of the color, smell, temperature, and sound of Stephen's surroundings. Trace the language of the senses in this chapter. How does Joyce use repeating sense-images to characterize Clongowes or Stephen's home in Dublin?

Chapter 2

New Characters:

Mike Flynn: *Stephen's running coach*

Aubrey Mills: *Stephen's friend in Blackrock*

Maurice: *Stephen's younger brother*

Vincent Heron: *Stephen's friend and "rival" at Belvedere*

Wallis: *Heron's friend*

Mr. Tate: *Stephen's English teacher at Belvedere*

Boland and Nash: *Heron's two friends*

Doyle: *the director of the play Stephen is in at Belvedere*

Johnny Cashman: *an old friend of Simon Dedalus in Cork*

E--- C--- / Emma: *the girl Stephen secretly admires*

Summary

In the first section, the narrator says that Uncle Charles smokes his morning pipe in the outhouse, because Stephen's father finds the tobacco smell unbearable. The Dedalus family has now moved to Blackrock, a suburb of Dublin, and it is summer. Stephen is spending a lot of time with Uncle Charles, going around town doing errands, and practicing track running in the park with Mike Flynn, a friend of Stephen's father. After practice, they often go to chapel, where Charles prays piously, while Stephen sits respectfully. He would go on long walks every Sunday with his father and Uncle Charles, during which he would listen to them talk about politics

and family history. At night, he would read a translation of *The Count of Monte Cristo*. The hero of this book, Edmond Dantes, appeals to Stephen, and he imagines his own life to be heroic and romantic. He has become friends with a boy named Aubrey Mills. They have formed a gang, and play adventure games together, in which Stephen, rather than dressing in a costume, makes a point of imitating Napoleon's plain style of dress.

In September, Stephen does not go back to Clongowes because his father cannot afford to send him. Mike Flynn is in the hospital, and Aubrey is at school, so Stephen starts driving around with the milkman on his route. His family's wealth is declining, and Stephen begins to imagine a female figure, such as Mercedes in *The Count of Monte Cristo*, who will transfigure and save him from the plainness of his life.

In the next section, the family has moved from Blackrock back to the city, and most of their furniture has just been reposessed by Mr. Dedalus' creditors. Stephen understands that his father is in trouble, but does not know the details. Uncle Charles has gotten too old to go outside, so Stephen explores Dublin on his own. He visits relatives with his mother, but continues to feel bitter and aloof. After a children's party, he takes the last tram home with the girl he admires. They stand near each other and, though they remain silent, Stephen feels a kind of connection with her. He thinks that she wants him to hold and kiss her, but he hesitates. The next day, he tries to write a poem to her. In the poem, he alters some of the details from the previous night—they are under trees rather than on a tram, and at the "moment of farewell," this time, they kiss.

One night, Stephen learns that his father has arranged for him and his brother, Maurice, to attend Belvedere College, another Jesuit school. His father then recounts, at dinner, how Father Conmee told him about Stephen going to speak to him about Father Dolan. Mr. Dedalus imitates Father Conmee saying they had a "hearty laugh together over it."

In the next section, Stephen is near the end of his second year at Belvedere. It is the night of the school play, and Stephen has the leading role in the second section, playing a comical teacher. Stephen, impatient with the first act, goes out of the chapel where

the play is being staged. He encounters two of his classmates—Heron and Wallis—smoking outside. Heron urges Stephen to imitate the rector of Belvedere in the play. Heron says that he saw Stephen's father going in, and teases him because Emma was with him. Their jesting makes Stephen angry and uncomfortable, but this mood soon passes. As they jokingly implore him to "admit" that he is "no saint," Stephen plays along, reciting the *Confiteor.*

While doing so, Stephen's mind wanders to a time, about a year back, when his writing teacher had found a mild example of heresy in one of his essays. Stephen does not argue, but corrects his error. A few days later, however, Heron and two others stop him and tease him about it, asking him who the "greatest writer" and "best poet" are. When Stephen says that Byron is the best poet, Heron mocks him, calling Byron a heretic. They hold Stephen and hit him with a cane and cabbage stump, telling him to "admit that Byron was no good."

Remembering the incident now, he is not angry. He is thinking of the fact that Emma will be in the audience, and he tries to remember what she looks like. A younger student comes up and tells Stephen he'd better hurry back and dress for the play.

He goes back in and gets his face painted for the part. He is not nervous, though he is humiliated by the silliness of the part he has to play. The play goes well, and Stephen leaves in a hurry as soon as it is over. Seeing his family outside, and noting that Emma is not with them, he leaves ahead of them—angry, frustrated, and restless.

In the next section, Stephen is on a train to Cork with his father. Cork is the city where Simon Dedalus grew up. They are traveling now because the Dedalus' properties are going to be sold. His father tells stories about his youth in Cork, but Stephen listens without sympathy or pity. In Cork, Mr. Dedalus asks just about everyone they meet about local news, and people he used to know, which makes Stephen restless and impatient. While visiting the Queen's College, Stephen becomes depressed looking at the carvings on the desks, imagining the lives of the students. His father finds his own initials, carved years ago, which only depresses Stephen further.

Hearing his father tell more stories, Stephen thinks of his own position at Belvedere. His father gives him advice, to "always mix with gentlemen," and reminisces about his own father. Stephen is

ashamed of his father, and thinks that the people they meet are condescending and patronizing. He feels distant from the world of his father, and the section ends with Stephen repeating to himself lines from Shelley's poem, "To The Moon."

In the final section, Stephen has won 33 pounds in an essay competition. He takes his parents to dinner, telling his mother not to worry about the cost. He orders fruits and groceries, takes people to the theater, gives gifts, and spends his money generously, if unwisely. His "season of pleasure," however, doesn't last long, and soon life returns to normal. He is dismayed that he was unable to stop the family's decline, which causes him so much shame.

He begins to wander the seedy parts of Dublin, this time searching for a woman to sin with, rather than for the Mercedes-figure from the start of the chapter. At the close of the chapter, he has his first encounter with a prostitute. She seduces him, and Stephen's reaction is passive and submissive.

Analysis

After the dramatic ending of the first chapter, which closes with Stephen winning the approval of his classmates, the beginning of this chapter might be something of a let-down. Rather than immediately continuing Stephen's story, the narrative spends the first page or so describing seemingly banal, incidental, and trivial details about how Uncle Charles goes out to the outhouse to smoke his tobacco, because Stephen's father can't stand the smell. The tone of this chapter, as it begins, suggests routinization, habit—rather than presenting singular events, the narrator describes what Uncle Charles would do "every morning," or what he and Stephen would do "on week days." The long and ultimately circular walks Stephen takes, every Sunday, with his father and Uncle Charles, suggest how much his life has become a progression of routines, and how much his freedom is limited by the adult world once again, Though he is no longer at Clongowes, he is still, to some degree, at the disposal of adult authority. His literal, physical freedom is limited, and his means of escape, throughout this chapter, becomes imaginative.

This juxtaposition of a dramatic moment at the end of one chapter, and a tone of routinization which tends to deflate that climax at the start of the next chapter, initiates a pattern that will

continue throughout the novel. Each chapter will characteristically end with an energetic climax, a moment of enlightenment for Stephen, while the next chapter, as it begins, will seem to show that this moment may not have been as significant as we had thought. This might suggest that the narrator, despite his close engagement with Stephen's perspective, has a tendency to ironize or parody aspects of his youthful triumphs. It may be that we feel that we can see or know more than Stephen, as Stephen is so young that he does not know all he thinks he does. This is the case throughout the novel, though it is perhaps less obvious as he gets older. The narrator always asks us to consider Stephen in a critical light, even when the language of the narration seems to be wholeheartedly affirming him.

This point is made especially specific in the second chapter, as we (and Stephen) hear Mr. Dedalus recount, over dinner, an encounter with Father Conmee, the rector at Clongowes. He retells the story, which had seemed like such an unambiguous triumph for young Stephen at the end of the previous chapter, in a patronizing, almost ridiculing tone:

> …we were chatting away quite friendly and he asked me did our friend here wear glasses still and then he told me the whole story.
> —And was he annoyed, Simon?
> —Annoyed! Note he! *Manly little chap!* he said.
> Mr Dedalus imitated the mincing nasal tone of the provincial.
> —Father Dolan and I, when I told them all at dinner about it, Father Dolan and I had a great laugh over it. You *better mind yourself, Father Dolan,* said I, or *young Dedalus will send you up for twice nine.* We had a famous laugh together over it. Ha! Ha! Ha!

Stephen's great act of self-assertion, heroism and confidence is reduced here to a comic anecdote; the champion of justice and the Roman people and senate is here reduced to a "manly little chap." While this passage is on the one hand, evidence of his father's insensitivity to his son—we will tend to sympathize with Stephen here—it will also cause us to reconsider the dramatic ending of the previous chapter in a different light.

One important effect of this moment for Stephen, we imagine, is upon his trust in authority. The confidence which he thought he shared with Father Conmee has been betrayed. Rather than reprimanding Father Dolan for his unfair treatment, the two joked about Stephen together. Throughout the second chapter, Stephen becomes more suspicious of authority figures. He has matured in many ways from the naive young boy of the first chapter. He is older now, and living in a different place—Blackrock, a suburb of Dublin. The spatial and temporal distance from Clongowes mirrors the other ways in which he has grown apart from his earlier life.

A telling example of this change in Stephen's attitude occurs early in the chapter, as he is training with Mike Flynn, an old friend of his father:

> Though he had heard his father say that Mike Flynn had put some of the best runners of modern times through his hands Stephen often glanced with mistrust at his trainer's flabby stubblecovered face, as it bent over the long stained fingers through which he rolled his cigarette, and with pity at the mild lusterless blue eyes which would look up suddenly from the task and gaze vaguely into the blue distance....

Contrast this mistrustful and suspicious attitude toward his father's recommended running trainer with the way Stephen asserts throughout the first chapter what "father said," or "Dante said," or "Uncle Charles said." There is a subtle sense of arrogance in the way Stephen looks "with pity" upon the man who is his trainer, his elder, and a close friend of his father. However, we must remember that, despite these changes in Stephen's attitude, he is still at the disposal of adult authority—there is no indication that Stephen is enrolled in track training because he wants to be. Although Mike Flynn's style of running—"his head high lifted, his knees well lifted and his hands held straight down by his sides"—seems antiquated and absurd to Stephen, he complies nonetheless.

Stephen's attitude toward religion, which is of course closely related to his attitude toward adult authority in general, is also changing as he gets older. This too is evident early on in the chapter, as Stephen visits the chapel with Uncle Charles. While Charles prays habitually and piously, Stephen is respectful, "though he did not share [Charles'] piety":

> He often wondered what his granduncle prayed for so
> seriously. Perhaps he prayed for the souls of purgatory or for
> the grace of a happy death or perhaps he prayed that God
> might send him back a part of the big fortune he squandered
> in Cork.

Stephen not only does not understand his uncle's religious belief, the familiar questioning tone which we recognize from the first chapter has now a sharper, subtly sarcastic edge. By suggesting that Charles might be praying for God to "send him back" the fortune he "squandered," Stephen is not only making a critique of Charles' religious faith (equating the selfless prayers with the selfish), but expressing his dissatisfaction with the family's declining economic status. This suggests the extent to which he is beginning to blame his father and Charles for being careless.

Stephen's faith in authority has weakened. He assumes a highly critical, almost arrogant, attitude toward those in a position of authority. His father is in serious economic trouble. Father Conmee has betrayed his confidence. Stephen is at once betrayed by and disappointed in various figures of authority in his life, while at the same time he begins to assume such roles himself. He is the leader of the boys' gang in their adventure games, fashioning himself after Napoleon. He is the leader of his class. He has been elected secretary of the gymnasium. He even assumes the paternal role of economic provider when he distributes the prize money from the essay contest.

Stephen is quick to set himself apart from his peers and to assume responsibility himself. As the day-to-day circumstances of his life become more dreary, and as the family is continually forced to move and to sell its property, Stephen's hopes become pinned to some kind of deliverance. His attitude throughout the chapter is a kind of restless expectation, an impatience with his prosaic surroundings, and a reliance upon his increasingly poetic imagination. More than once we are told of his sense of destiny, how he feels greater things are in store for him, and that his hardship is only temporary. While he listens to his father and Uncle Charles talk about Irish politics, history, and folktales, Stephen is silent, but intrigued.

The life that has seemed so incomprehensible to him in the first chapter now seems like a world of not-too-distant potential. However, it soon becomes clear that this is not a matter of following in his father's and Charles' footsteps; Stephen's sense of uniqueness and potential moves him away from his family's plight, and into the "intangible fantasies" of his own mind.

Stephen's increasingly critical attitude toward authority does not lead to a spirit of conflict. Rather, he assumes a pose of detachment. As when Uncle Charles was praying, and Stephen has an air of what we could call "respectful" silence, he feels a disengaged dissatisfaction with his family's declining wealth. When he feels that his father expects his support, that he "was being enlisted for the fight" his family was going to have with its creditors, Stephen's reaction is to remain as detached as possible, to think again of the future.

The change in the family's situation has clearly changed Stephen's perception of the world: "For some time he had felt the slight changes in his house; and those changes in what he had deemed unchangeable were so many slight shocks to his boyish conception of the world." This shaking of his faith in his father's stability results, in part, in a suspicion of his father, and in a sense that he must try to become more independent. He begins to consciously assume and accept the role of the exile or pariah that he was uncomfortable with in the first chapter.

Stephen's pose of detachment, then, does not lead to any direct rebellion at this point. Unlike Heron, his classroom rival who delights in bullying younger students and disrespecting the teachers (at least behind their backs), Stephen does not sway from his "quiet obedience." Amidst all the worldly voices surrounding him at school and at home, Stephen pins his hopes on his imagination. He begins to look at his present surroundings as temporary—he is trapped by circumstance, but feels that he will be able to be free soon. His longings are of course heavily colored by the literature he reads. Literature, for Stephen, provides a means of escape from the reality of his surroundings. While reading *The Count of Monte Cristo,* he fancies himself the dark romantic hero, proud in his exile. He imagines his wanderings through the city as a "quest" for a figure like Mercedes, who would have the power to "transfigure" him, at which time "weakness and timidity and inexperience would fall from him."

This idealized Mercedes—which of course doesn't connect with anything in Stephen's experience—forms his attitude toward Emma, and women more generally, throughout the novel. Emma or "E---C---," is rarely mentioned by name in the novel. She is most often referred to as "her" or "she," which is significant because it shows how Stephen reduces her to a symbolic, and highly literary, "woman-figure" rather than perceiving her as a thinking and feeling person in her own right. She functions for Stephen, throughout the novel, more as an idea than as an actual person. As he imagines her waiting in the audience at the play, and is anxious and apparently in love, it is telling that he cannot even recall what she looks like: "He tried to recall her appearance but could not. He could only remember that she had worn a shawl about her head like a cowl and that her dark eyes had invited and unnerved him." It is telling that, as Stephen tries to recall something about her appearance, his mind reverts immediately to the effect she had on him.

Our perspective, as with everywhere else in the novel, is limited to Stephen, and in the case of Emma we sense this acutely. How different, we imagine, would Emma's account of their ride on the tram be? Whenever Stephen is obsessing over her, we cannot but suspect that here, as elsewhere, his imagination is largely responsible. It is significant that Emma is hard to distinguish from other female figures in the novel, such as Eileen, his childhood friend, and Mercedes, for whom he searches the city. Stephen treats women as symbolic and abstract figures in his life, and not as actualities. Therefore, this "image" will always be in conflict with the actuality of her behavior. In the second chapter and throughout the novel, we suspect that Emma would be surprised by Stephen's descriptions and fantasies. We wonder, with him, whether he is present in her mind at all. However, we hesitate to assign to her any "unfaithfulness" for this as he does. Given the scarcity of their actual contact, it is quite reasonable that she doesn't think of him.

This situation is illustrated nowhere better than in the poem Stephen composes for her. This is our first glimpse at an attempt of artistic creation on Stephen's part. The narrator mentions an attempt, after the Christmas dinner in the first chapter, when Stephen tried to write a poem about Parnell, but couldn't because "his brain had then refused to grapple with the theme." This time,

Stephen succeeds in composing a poem, though we do not get to see it. This suggests, given the selectivity of this narrative, that the circumstances surrounding the act of creation are more important than the product of its labors. He is inspired by the incident on the late night tram with Emma, and his poem is supposedly written for her.

Stephen's composition is highly formal—he seems more enamored of the idea of writing a poem than of the poem itself. He entitles it before he starts writing, and is sure to draw an "ornamental line" underneath the title. His paper is headed with the Jesuit motto, "A.M.D.G." *("Ad Majerum Dei Gloriam"),* and at the foot of the page he writes another motto, "L.D.S." *("Laus Deo Semper").* His title shows how much he sees himself as working within a tradition of English poetry. He titles it "To E--- C---," asserting that "He knew it was right to begin so for he had seen similar titles in the collected poems of Lord Byron." The influence of Byron, however, is as superficial as the Jesuit mottoes, which he includes "from force of habit." It is as if all these extraneous, decorative surroundings—the title, the ornamental line, the Jesuit mottoes, the new bottle of ink, new pen, and new notebook—all get in the way of his creation.

It is no surprise, then, that once he is able to compose his poem (after a brief daydream), that it is as removed as possible from the scene the night before which inspired it. Stephen uses his art to transform and obscure reality, while improving on it. If he hesitates to kiss her in life, he doesn't in the poem. Just as his way of dealing with his family's financial trouble is to detach himself, his way of escaping the "squalor" of his life is to engage in imaginative fantasy. His poem serves just this purpose. Just as his interest in Emma is more in the idea of a female-figure in his life, his interest in poetry, at this point, is more in the idea of being a poet. It is personal and private—he hides the book, and as far as we know doesn't show anyone. Art for Stephen, at this point, is another means of escape and detachment from reality.

Language, throughout this chapter, continues to be fascination for Stephen, and a key aspect of the way his mind works (and, consequently, of the way this narrative works). Consider how, when Heron and Wallis are harassing him, it is the word "Admit!" which sets his mind off on the long digression about the time his English teacher accused him of heresy. This memory is spurred by this "familiar word of admonition"—he recalls how that time, too, Heron had tried to force him to "admit" that Byron is a heretic. The logic of this narrative is associative, and such transitions and digressions are justified by the associations in Stephen's mind. As we noted in the previous chapter, these are frequently linguistic.

This capacity for a word to spawn a virtual mental flood for Stephen is not simply limited to cases of memory, however. While visiting Queen's College in Cork with his father, he sees the word *Foetus* carved into a desk. Its effect on Stephen is instantaneous:

> The sudden legend startled his blood: he seemed to feel the absent students of the college about him and to shrink from their company. A vision of their life, which his father's words had been powerless to evoke, sprang up before him out of the word cut in the desk.

Words in their active application do not have this kind of force for Stephen—his father's constant descriptions and anecdotes about his school days had bored and annoyed Stephen. But this word, carved into a desk and removed from any active or purposeful use, brings the scene immediately to life. It is as if this potential resides somewhere in the word itself.

As we soon learn, the force of this experience is greater because this word and its associations—which for Stephen are primarily sexual—resonate with his own life. Stephen experiences normal, adolescent, sexual awakening as a profoundly singular, abnormal, "brutish and individual malady." We learn that the reason that the word *Foetus* has such an effect on him is because it shocks him that other boys would think about the same "monstrous" things as he does. Again, Stephen tends to see his own experience as unique—he shies from any deep connection with others, and thus assumes that he is the only one who feels as he does. We could also read Stephen's hyperbolic reaction as a critique of Catholic teaching on adolescent sexuality—despite his pose of singularity and uniqueness, we know that Stephen did not get the idea that this is "monstrous" on his own.

Stephen's somewhat excessive reaction here is typical, especially in this chapter. As we have noted, he tends to romanticize his life, and has begun to relish the role of the sensitive and mis-understood exile. If at times Stephen seems to overdramatize him-self, the narrator certainly has a role in this. As we saw earlier, this narrator is trying to mirror, through language, aspects of Stephen's personality as it develops. Throughout Chapter Two, his language is often somewhat excessive and melodramatic, to mirror Stephen's tendencies to view himself in this light. The narrative participates, with a seemingly straight face, in Stephen's posturings, presenting them as it were at face value. But do we take Stephen seriously throughout this chapter? Or might the narrator, by choosing such extreme language, be subtly parodying him?

When the narrator describes Stephen as answering Heron "urbanely," "Might I ask what you are talking about?," are we to understand that 16-year-old Stephen was "really" more urbane and sophisticated than his rude classmate, or that he was *acting* this way, putting on airs? His pretentious, elevated style of speech is not lost on Heron, anyway, who responds, "Indeed you might." Throughout this chapter, it seems that the narrator will participate in Stephen's posturings, using excessive or melodramatic language to describe his stance or tone of voice, while subtly undercutting him, or inviting us to be critical of him.

Like Stephen's poem, the narrator's language, by "participating" in Stephen's state of mind to this degree, often renders it difficult to distinguish exactly what is happening. For example, near the end of the chapter, after Stephen had squandered his money and has taken to wandering the seedy areas of Dublin at night, the narrator tells of his "shameful" and "secret riots." Only after a very close reading does it become clear that these are only in his mind, and that his encounter with the prostitute at the close of the chapter is his first. The narrator distorts the actuality in a similar way as Stephen himself does—we are to understand, after the *Foetus* episode, that he experiences his sexuality and fantasies in this extreme manner. The narrator is attempting to replicate and reflect the state of Stephen's mind; by doing so, he often participates in the same kind of distortions as Stephen.

Throughout this chapter, Stephen sets himself as far apart as possible from his surroundings. His family and his city are a source of shame, and the binary between fantasy and reality is operative throughout the chapter. Stephen begins to assume the role of the exile, modeling himself after Lord Byron and Edmond Dantes from *The Count of Monte Cristo*. He has a vague sense of a "calling," some "special purpose" for his life, though it is not yet clear what this will be. He sets himself apart from the other students at the school, and from the members of his family; he is convinced that he is unique. However, in many ways the narrative seems to suggest that Stephen might not be as different as he thinks. The fact that other boys his age have and have always had sexual fantasies comes as an absolute shock to him. He characterizes his sexuality in extreme, abnormal terms but the narrator seems to suggest that it is not as strange as he might think. And, although he criticizes his father and Uncle Charles for their irresponsibility with money, Stephen's excess and carelessness with his prize money shows us that he might not be as far from his father's world as he would like to think. He assumes the role of paternal provider, to try "to build a breakwater of order and elegance against the sordid tide of life," but realizes, of course, that he cannot sustain it. Alongside all of Stephen's assertions that he is a unique figure, the narrative continues to suggest ways he is not.

Study Questions

1. Where is the Dedalus family living at the start of the chapter?
2. What does Stephen read alone in his room at night?
3. Why does Stephen not return to Clongowes in September?
4. When the family has moved back to Dublin, why does Stephen spend so much time alone?
5. Why does Stephen feel it is appropriate to entitle his poem, "To E--- C---"?
6. Where does Stephen go to school after Clongowes?
7. Why does Heron mock Byron, who Stephen says is "the best poet"?
8. What word does Stephen see carved on a desk at Queen's College in Cork?
9. Where does Stephen get the money for his "season of pleasure"?

10. How does Stephen react to the prostitute at the end of the chapter?

Answers

1. The family has moved to Blackrock, a suburb on the coast southeast of Dublin.

2. Stephen reads a translation of *The Count of Monte Cristo* by Alexandre Dumas.

3. Stephen is unable to return to Clongowes because his father can no longer afford to send him.

4. Stephen spends so much time alone in Dublin because he has few friends, and his Uncle Charles has gotten too old to go outside.

5. Stephen imitates the titles of some poems he has seen in the collected works of Lord Byron, the English Romantic poet.

6. Stephen is sent to Belvedere College by special arrangement by Father Conmee, Stephen's former rector at Clongowes. Conmee is now at Belvedere, and arranges for Stephen and his brother Maurice to attend the Jesuit academy.

7. Heron says that Byron was a heretic.

8. Stephen sees the word *"Foetus"* carved in the desk in the lecture hall at Queen's College.

9. Stephen wins 33 pounds in an essay competition, which he spends lavishly and generously, if quickly and irresponsibly.

10. Stephen's reaction to the prostitute is passive and submissive.

Suggested Essay Topics

1. Stephen's attitude toward authority and authority figures undergoes some important changes in Chapter Two. Discuss some ways in which Stephen's behavior in this chapter contrasts with his behavior in the first chapter. Examine specific scenes and passages where this contrast is evident.

2. Throughout Chapter Two, we learn much about Stephen's attitude toward women. From the Mercedes-figure in the early pages to the prostitute at the end, we see his idea and ideal of women develop. Compare and contrast the female-figures in the novel (Mercedes, Emma, the prostitutes) and the place they hold in Stephen's imaginative life.

3. In what ways does this narrator seem to undercut Stephen's sense of uniqueness and singularity? Examine some scenes where it seems that the narrator takes an ironic view toward Stephen.

SECTION FOUR

Chapter 3

New Characters:

Ennis: *a classmate of Stephen's at Belvedere*

Old Woman: *in the street, who directs Stephen to the chapel*

Priest: *at the Church Street chapel where Stephen confesses*

Summary

Stephen has now made a habit of visiting brothels. In school, he is bored and uninspired, and the narrative details the wanderings of his mind while he sits in class. He is not plagued by guilt for his sins, but rather feels a "cold lucid indifference." He feels that he is beyond salvation, and can do nothing to control his lust. He has begun to despise his fellow students, in part because of what he sees as an empty and hypocritical piety on their part. He serves as prefecture of the sodality of the Blessed Virgin Mary—a highly esteemed religious organization at Belvedere—but feels no guilt at the "falsehood of his position." He sometimes considers confessing to the members of the sodality, but feels such contempt for them that he does not.

After the math class is over, the other students urge Stephen to try and stall the teacher of the next class by asking difficult questions about the catechism. Before the religion class, Stephen enjoys contemplating the theological dilemmas. When the rector comes in, he announces that a religious retreat in honor of St. Francis Xavier will begin on Wednesday afternoon. He tells the class about Francis Xavier's life—he was one of the first followers of

Ignatius, the Founder of the Jesuit order. He spends his career converting pagans in the Indies, Africa and Asia, and is known for the great number of converts he amassed. Stephen anticipates the coming retreat with anxiety and fear.

In the next section, Stephen is at the retreat. Father Arnall is giving an introductory sermon, which causes Stephen to remember his days at Clongowes. Father Arnall welcomes the boys, and speaks of the tradition of this retreat. He talks of the boys who have done it in years past, and wonders where they are now. He explains the significance and importance of a periodic retreat from ordinary life, and says that during the retreat they will be taught about the "four last things": death, judgment, hell, and heaven. He encourages them to clear their minds of worldly thoughts, and to attend to their souls. Father Arnall claims that this retreat will have a profound impact on their lives.

After dinner, it is clear that the promise of the next four days has already had an effect on Stephen—he perceives himself as a "beast," and begins to feel fear.

This fear becomes "a terror of spirit" as the sermon makes Stephen think of his own death and judgment in morbid detail. This leads him to consider Doomsday, the final judgment. The sermon affects Stephen deeply and personally, and he feels how his "soul was festering in sin."

Walking home, he hears a girl laughing, which causes him intense shame. He thinks of Emma, and is ashamed as he imagines how she would react to his lifestyle. He imagines repenting, and her forgiving him, and he imagines the Virgin Mary simultaneously marrying and forgiving the both of them. It is raining, and Stephen thinks of the biblical flood.

Next, we hear a sermon which solidifies Stephen's conviction that he must repent. Beginning with Creation and Original Sin, the sermon reaches the story of Jesus and the importance of repentance and God's forgiveness. Then follows a lengthy and detailed description of the torments of hell and damnation—it is a physical and geographical account of hell, and a graphic depiction of the bodily and psychological torments hell inflicts on the damned.

As he leaves the chapel, Stephen is greatly upset by the sermon. He fears hell and death, and decides that there is still time to

change his life. In class, Stephen's thoughts are saturated with the language of the sermon. When confessions are being heard, Stephen feels that he must confess, but wonders if he can. He decides that he cannot confess in the college chapel, but must go elsewhere.

That night, the sermon focuses upon the spiritual torments of hell. It details how the damned have a full awareness of what they have lost, and that their conscience will continue to plague them with guilt. He reminds the boys of the eternity of hell, and describes how the awareness of this would torment the damned. He describes sin as a personal affront to Jesus, and the sermon ends with a prayer of repentance, which Stephen takes to heart.

After dinner, Stephen goes up to his room to pray, still feeling the effects of the sermon. He thinks about his sins, and feels surprised that God has allowed him to live this long. With his eyes closed, he has a vision of hell—Stephen's hell is a land of dry thistle and weed, solid excrement, dim light, and goat-like, half-human creatures who mumble and circle around him. His vision of hell sickens and frightens him. He almost faints, then vomits, and, weakened, he prays.

In the evening, he leaves the house, looking to confess his sins, but is scared that he won't be able to. Seeing some poor girls sitting on the side of the street, Stephen is ashamed at the thought that their souls are dearer to God than his. He asks an old woman where the nearest chapel is, and she directs him.

Inside the Church St. Chapel, he kneels at the last bench. Once the priest arrives and the other people in the chapel begin going in for confession, Stephen has second thoughts. When his turn comes, however, he goes in almost automatically. Inside the confessional, he recites the *Confiteor,* and tells the priest that it has been eight months since his last confession. First he confesses more minor sins—masses he missed, prayers not said—then gradually reaches his "sins of impurity." He tells the priest all the details. When the priest asks how old he is, Stephen answers, "sixteen." The priest implores Stephen to repent and to change his lifestyle, suggesting that he pray to the Virgin Mary when he is tempted. The priest blesses him, and Stephen prays fervently.

On his way home, Stephen is ecstatic, feeling an inner peace in his life. In the morning, he takes communion with his classmates.

The ritual affects Stephen deeply, and he feels that a new life has begun for him.

Analysis

Once again, the chapter begins with a sense of dull routine. The excitement of his transgression, which had ended Chapter Two is here deflated—there is no indication of any sense of thrill or danger in Stephen's now frequent visits to the brothels. Instead, they have become as dull and ordinary for him as the rest of the Dublin society from which he seeks to distance himself. Stephen's attempts to set himself apart from his surroundings seem frustrated—the narrator is showing us, at the start of this chapter, that perhaps Stephen's experience with the prostitute was not the significant transformative experience that he had thought.

The verb tense throughout the opening paragraphs, as Stephen is in class thinking of the night to come, suggests just how much of a habit this has become for him:

> It would be a gloomy secret night. After early nightfall the yellow lamps would light up, here and there, the squalid quarter of the brothels. He would follow a devious course up and down the streets....

Clearly, this "gloomy secret night" will not differ greatly from any other night of the week for Stephen. Visiting the brothels seems to have become as much a part of his daily routine as school.

However, the fact that this habit has lost its charge of excitement for Stephen is made clear by the narrator's use of light imagery, which characterizes Stephen's present life as dull, dusky, and dim:

> The swift December dusk had come tumbling clownishly after its dull day and, as he started through the dull square window of the schoolroom, he felt his belly crave for its food.

The repetition of "dull" and "dusk" throughout the opening pages of the chapter suggests both habit and stasis, while the metaphorical language of dusk and dullness suggests just how plain and unappealing Stephen's lifestyle has become for him.

In a sense, this first paragraph represents Stephen's moral state at the start of this chapter. Chapter Three is thematically concerned

with Stephen's moral and religious state, which undergoes a major transformation over the course of the five days covered by the chapter. As the chapter opens, he is in class daydreaming about dinner:

> He hoped there would be stew for dinner, turnips and carrots and bruised potatoes and fat mutton pieces to be ladled out in thick peppered flourfattened sauce. Stuff it into you, his belly counselled him.

His intellect, or spirit, is subsumed in favor of his bodily appetites, a clear echo of the lustful nature of his sin. That this sin has become dull and unappealing in itself is suggested by the quality of food Stephen expects: bruised, fat, thick, and flourfattened. He does not indicate that there is something about the food itself which appeals to him. Rather, its chief quality that is that it will satisfy a bodily need, evidenced by the crudity of the phrase, "stuff it into you." Stephen is now motivated by the physical and worldly—his "belly" is personified as an entity separate from and dominant over his mind. His lust for food is clearly associated with his sexual lust, as his mind seems to progress naturally from thinking about dinner to thinking about wandering the brothel district. Both cravings are equally devoid of feeling.

As the novel's central chapter, Chapter Three is the most temporally and thematically focused and concentrated. Whereas the other chapters in the novel cover anywhere from a few months to a few years in Stephen's life, Chapter Three intensely focuses on five crucial days. Even within these five days, the narrative excludes everything except what specifically concerns Stephen's spiritual and religious status. We have the impression that this retreat consists only of Stephen hearing sermons, then cowering in his room, and eventually walking across town for confession. While he surely did many other things during these days, this narrator is interested only in presenting the details essential to the development of Stephen's soul. Therefore, the focus of the narrative in this chapter is intensely concentrated.

John Blades describes it as a "chapter of excesses." Father Arnall's sermons are excessive in their scope, and in their morbid and explicit attention to detail. The narrative is excessive in its unrelenting and comprehensive presentation of these sermons.

It shifts from direct quotation of the priest to the style of paraphrase that seems to present Stephen's reactions to the sermon at the same time, but our overall impression of this section of the chapter is like sitting through these entire sermons. There is very little narrative presence interrupting the relentless flow of the priest's words. Stephen's response is also somewhat excessive, feeling that "every word was for him," and fearing an immediate death at the hand of God on his way back to his room.

One important change in Stephen's character in this chapter is in his attitude toward his peers. What we recognize in Chapter Two as a pose of detachment has now become a more explicit "contempt" for his peers. He perceives their acts of piety and religious devotion as hypocritical, easy and shallow, and feels no shame about his "double life" around them. The pose of exile and detachment here takes on a distinctly sinful quality—pride. This is an extreme manifestation of his feelings of uniqueness and exile in Chapter Two, and one which suggests the sinful state of his soul. The restlessness and impatience with the world of his family and his classmates, and the pervasive hope that some great calling awaits him, has now become a "cold lucid indifference" toward his own soul, and toward the extent to which he continues to live in sin.

While Stephen tries to convince himself that he is indifferent to his sin, and feels no regret or discomfort with "the falsehood of his position" as prefect of the sodality of the Blessed Virgin Mary, it is clear that he has been not able to escape the influence of the Catholic church. First of all, his sinful lifestyle does to constitute a rejection of or loss of belief in God:

> What did it avail to pray when he knew that his soul lusted after its own destruction? A certain pride, a certain awe, withheld him from offering to God even one prayer at night though he knew it was in God's power to take away his life while he slept and hurl his soul hellward ere he could beg for mercy.

Stephen seems to fashion himself here after Milton's Satan; we can sense a romantic pleasure in his defiance of God's power. For Stephen never expresses disbelief of or lack of faith in God, and he is still intimately familiar with the tenents of the Catholic faith (evidenced by his role as resident expert in his class on obscure questions about the catechism). Stephen seems to take both pride and morbid and masochistic pleasure in his deep theological knowledge:

> It was strange too that he found an arid pleasure in following up to the end of rigid lines of the doctrines of the church and penetrating into obscure silences only to hear and feel the more deeply his own condemnation.

His interest in the details of Catholic doctrine has a certain detached quality—as if religion were a series of puzzling intellectual questions and obscure knowledge. At the same time, however, Stephen seems to find a certain thrill in applying the consequences of these doctrines to his own sinful life. He is deeply aware of the "letter of the law," but this awareness never translates into a reaction to the "spirit of the law" until after the retreat. His interest in theological questions bears a very limited connection to his daily life. Up to this point, Stephen's relationship to the church is both an idle intellectual game, and a useful romantic trope for his imaginative construction of his own life.

Though he manages to remain detached to this degree, he is never outside of the structures of the church. He always refers to his "sin" and to his "condemnation," terms that have no application outside of the framework of religious doctrine and belief. By identifying his behavior as a "sin," and by dwelling on it to this degree, we can see how much the language and beliefs of the Catholic church continue to have a hold on him. We can see, from the start of the chapter, just how ripe Stephen is to be swayed by the sermon.

The centerpiece of this chapter is the pair of sermons Father Arnall gives concerning hell and damnation. He quite literally puts "the fear of God" into Stephen, who, at the end of the chapter, repents, confesses, and begins a new life in the service of God. The narrator, as a recognizable presence, all but drops out of the picture in this section. Stephen speaks very little in this chapter, but listens and reacts internally to the sermon. The narrator is able to illustrate this by recreating Stephen's experience for the reader—we are made to listen to the sermon almost word-for-word, which recreates

Stephen's experience in the congregation, continuing to align us exclusively with his perspective.

Although the narrative starts by quoting large portions of the sermon, we soon are able to recognize many characteristics of Father Arnall's language in the narrator's "own" narration, paraphrasing to the extent that the narrator's voice sounds like the priest's:

> At the last moment of consciousness the whole earthly life passed before the vision of the soul and, ere it had time to reflect, the body had died and the soul stood terrified before the judgement seat. God, who had long been merciful, would then be just....

Eventually, the narration starts to present the sermon directly, but without quoting, and without the marks of paraphrase in its syntax. The two voices seem to have merged completely:

> And this day will come, shall come, must come; the day of death and the day of judgment. It is appointed unto man to die and after death the judgment. Death is certain. The time and manner are uncertain...

The narrator no longer seems to be telling us what the priest said, so much as saying it directly. Our close alignment with Stephen's perspective allows us to "experience" this sermon more or less from his position as an audience member in the congregation.

The priest's rhetoric becomes the "action" of this chapter. Since Stephen is convinced that "every word was for him," when we read the narrator's paraphrase of the sermon, we are able to gauge Stephen's reaction at the same time. Father Arnall, who presumably gives the sermon (since he is running the retreat), is named initially before being reduced to "the priest." He eventually recedes as a direct presence in the narrative altogether. His language becomes, then, much less personalized, underscoring just how much Stephen is tending to take this as God's direct word, and as an unadulterated voice of absolute authority.

Stephen's reaction to the sermon, then, represents a kind of regression. Throughout Chapter Two, as we recognized, Stephen was becoming increasingly suspicious of authority figures. In the early section of Chapter Three, as his classmates are encouraging him to stall the teacher with a series of obscure and difficult theological questions, we are reminded of his lack of deep regard for authority. However, throughout Chapter Three, he becomes less critical and more accepting of the authority of the clergy, represented by Father Arnall at the retreat, and the old priest at the chapel to whom Stephen confesses. His relationship to religion here is more emotional and simplistic. He does not question the authorities on the finer points of Catholic doctrine, but fears and respects them, and takes their words and their power directly to heart.

This is one of several ways in which Stephen's repentance represents a return to innocence. The reappearance of Father Arnall in the novel, whom we last saw in Chapter One, at Clongowes, recalls us to the time when Stephen was younger:

> The figure of his old master, so strangely rearisen, brought back to Stephen's mind his life at Clongowes: the wide playgrounds, swarming with boys, the square ditch, the little cemetery off the main avenue of limes where he had dreamed of being buried, the firelight on the wall of the infirmary where he lay sick, the sorrowful face of Brother Michael. His soul, as these memories came back to him, became again a child's soul.

Whereas in Chapter Two, Stephen was eager to distance himself from those days, when "the memory of his childhood [was] dim" and he could not "call forth...vivid moments" but "only names," seeing Father Arnall calls up vivid and detailed memories for Stephen. In a sense, these are "memories" for the reader, too, as they cause us to recall how Stephen was then. The very appearance of Father Arnall symbolizes how this retreat will be a return to a state of innocence for Stephen, who assumes a childlike openness as he listens to the sermon. The narrator's language at the end of the chapter, after Stephen has repented and confessed, recalls the more childlike rhythms of Chapter One:

> He had confessed and God had pardoned him. His soul was made fair and holy once more, holy and happy. It would be beautiful to die if God so willed. It was beautiful to live if God so willed, to live in grace a life of peace and virtue and forbearance with others.

The convention of the priest calling him "my child" takes on special significance, as Stephen's confession represents a revision to his more childlike submission to voices of authority.

If the effect of Stephen's repentance is a seeming return to a state of lost innocence, then the priest's sermon certainly contributes to this. Stephen's repentance and change of heart are motivated by fear more than anything else. The sermon focuses solely on the threat of the tortures of hell; the method is to intimidate the young boys into behaving according to the law of God. His reason for living a pious life never move beyond intimidation. He spends a large portion of his sermon describing hell's geographical and physical characteristics with quasi-scientific exactness, comparing hell's heat and fire to heat and fire on earth, trying to impress upon the boys in earthly terms the inconceivable and unearthly extremity and eternity of hell's torments. The priest never offers a positive reason to believe in and follow God, but rests his argument solely on the consequences of a sinful life.

His very poetic and imaginative reconstruction of hell appeals to Stephen's artistic sensibility rather than to his intellect. Stephen's remorse, then, is not moral or intellectual in character—it is motivated primarily by fear of hell, God's wrath, and eternal damnation. Like the omnipresent threat of pandying or flogging at Clongowes, hell functions as an intimidation tactic, divorced from any moral choice. In Chapter Three, Joyce seems to be making his most explicit critique of the Catholic church. Although the church functions throughout the novel as one of the primary fetters which Stephen Dedalus tries to free himself from, in this chapter its mechanisms are portrayed most explicitly as coercive, simplistic, and reductive.

Stephen's repentance and spiritual rebirth has an immediate effect on his attitude toward his peers. Walking home from confession, he is pleased "to live in grace a life of peace and virtue and forbearance with others." At communion the next day, he partakes humbly of the communal spirit of the ritual:

> The boys were all there, kneeling in their places. He knelt
> among them, happy and shy....
> He knelt before the altar with his classmates, holding the
> altar cloth with them over a living rail of hands.

Stephen seems to feel a connection with his peers for the first time in the novel. His alienation and insecurity, which he felt as a child, and his proud exile, which developed as an adolescent, all seem to be abandoned in favor of this feeling of brotherhood and connectedness.

Before his confession, however, Stephen's sense of detachment and singularity is still present. His reaction to the sermon is intensely personal—he interprets it as a personal message from God, and the narrator illustrates how Stephen's extreme reaction is unique among his classmates. After the first sermon, while Stephen is vividly imagining his own death and damnation, the other students' voices serve to undercut and deflate his personal drama:

> His flesh shrank together as it felt the approach of the ravenous tongues of flames, dried up as it felt about it the swirl of stifling air. He had died. Yes. He was judged. A wave of fire swept through his body: the first. Again a wave. His brain began to glow. Another. His brain was simmering and bubbling within the cracking tenement of the skull. Flames burst forth from his skull like a corolla, shrieking like voices:
>
> —Hell! Hell! Hell! Hell! Hell!
> Voices spoke near him:
> —On hell.
> —I suppose he rubbed it into you well.
> —You bet he did. He put us all into a blue funk.
> —That's what you fellows want: and plenty of it to make you work.

The sound, *like* voices, in Stephen's imagination is juxtaposed with the actual voices of Mr. Tate and Vincent Heron. The colloquial chattiness of their reaction—"he rubbed it into you," "you bet he did"— presents a plainer reality next to Stephen's imaginative life, suggesting that Stephen's egotism results in an overreaction on his part. Mr. Tate jokingly reduces the voice of God which has quaked Stephen's soul to a mere scare tactic to keep the students working. The narrator presents Stephen's experience of these things literally, physically, which furthers this sense of two separate realities here. Stephen's skull is melting, flames are shooting from his head, while Mr. Tate and Heron joke about the students being put into a "blue funk."

We might sense a tone of elitism or superiority in Stephen's reaction, if we keep in mind his attitude of contempt toward the other students' shows of piety earlier. It is easy to see how his reaction would seem, to him, as the "real" or "righteous" one, while theirs is shallow and trivial. The same kind of operative distinction between Stephen's imaginative reality and ordinary life, which characterized Chapter Two, is at work here. We can see, in this scene, Stephen's poetic and dramatic imagination coloring his experience as unique and incommunicable, participating in and contributing to his feeling of alienation.

His feelings of contempt and disdain for his peers might still be somewhat active as he decides that he must confess his sins, "but not there among his school companions." Ostensibly, his motive here is "shame" and "abjection of spirit"—he feels he is not worthy to confess in the college chapel among their "boyish hearts." Implicit in this humility, however, is the same kind of feeling of exile, detachment, and superiority which motivated his "contempt" for them earlier in the chapter. Stephen does not feel that he is a part of this community. Before, he had seen their "boyishness" as a limiting and infuriating immaturity. Now, however, he sees it as an innocence which he has lost.

As he is wandering the streets looking for a chapel, he sees "frowsy girls" along the side of the road. His "humiliation" that their souls may be dearer to God than his has its root in an implicit feeling of superiority or egotism. The implication, we suppose, is that he feels his soul should be dearer to God. Stephen's confession and repentance is motivated, in part, by a desire to change all this—while waiting his turn in the chapel, he is inspired by thinking about Jesus, and his love for the "poor and simple people." Before confession, Stephen's motivation is expressed thus:

> He would be at one with others and with God. He would love his neighbor. He would love God Who had made and loved him. He would kneel and pray with others and be happy. God would look down on him and on them and would love them all.

This communally oriented spirit is uncharacteristic of the Stephen we know. He seeks to identify himself with the group, to have his individual identity—which until now has been most important to him—subsumed under a group identity, and under God.

This represents another important reversion of the tendencies we recognized in Chapter Two. Stephen is trying to relinquish the role of exile he began to assume then. His confession and repentance is motivated by and seems to result in a feeling of brotherhood and communion with humanity. His religious rebirth "sets back the clock" in various ways. It represents a return to a state of innocence, reconciling his sins with God; it represents a new, less critical attitude toward authority, and a less hostile attitude toward his peers. Up to this point, Stephen's individual identity was most important, and he sought only to find some means of escape from ordinary Dublin life, but he now seems reconciled to his peers and to his environment. The image of Stephen wandering the dark streets to find a chapel near the end of Chapter Three is a clear echo of the end of Chapter Two, when he wanders the streets looking for a woman. Do we understand this as a kind of revision of this earlier scene, an attempt at starting over, this time on the "right foot"? Or do we hear an ironic echo of the earlier Stephen even here, suggesting that perhaps his change of heart is neither permanent nor desirable? He seems to have changed profoundly as Chapter Three closes—he seems happy to be a part of a "living rail of hands," to have conformed to the authority of God and the church. However, we should be suspicious, by now, of this novel's climaxes, and wonder, as we begin Chapter Four, whether this transformation is really for the better.

Study Questions

1. What is Stephen's attitude toward his sinful lifestyle as Chapter Three opens?

2. What religious office does Stephen hold at Belvedere?

3. What is important about St. Francis Xavier, according to the rector?

4. What are the "four last things" the sermons will cover during the retreat?

5. What effect does seeing Father Arnall have upon Stephen?

6. Why does Stephen feel he cannot confess at the college chapel?

7.   Describe Stephen's vision of hell.

8.   What effect does seeing the "frowsy girls" on the side of the road have on Stephen?

9.   How old is Stephen in Chapter Three?

10.   What does the priest tell Stephen after confession?

Answers

1.   Stephen claims to be indifferent; he does not feel shame or guilt around his classmates, and is too proud to pray to God and repent.

2.   Stephen is prefect of the sodality of the Blessed Virgin Mary.

3.   The rector tells the boys that St. Francis Xavier was one of the original Jesuits, one of the first followers of Ignatius. He was known for converting people in the Indies, Africa, and Asia. According to the rector, he once converted 10,000 in one month.

4.   The "four last things" are death, judgment, hell, and heaven. The topic of the sermons never reach heaven, as promised.

5.   Seeing Father Arnall recalls Stephen to his Clongowes days, making his soul "become again a child's soul," symbolizing how this retreat signifies a return to innocence for him.

6.   Stephen does not want to confess along with his classmates out of shame for the extent of his sins.

7.   Stephen imagines hell as peopled with goat-like, half-human creatures who encircle him, mumbling incoherently. It is a land of dry thistle and weeds, solid excrement, and dim light.

8.   When Stephen sees the poor girls, he is ashamed and humiliated at the thought that their souls are dearer to God than his.

9.   Stephen tells the priest during confession that he is 16 years old.

10.   The priest tells Stephen to resist the Devil's temptation, to repent, and to give up his life of sin. He tells Stephen to pray to the Virgin Mary when he is tempted.

Suggested Essay Topics

1. In many ways, Chapter Three represents a reversal of some of the tendencies Stephen developed in Chapter Two. Discuss the changes in his attitude toward authority figures, his peers, and his identity as an individual. In what ways does Stephen seem to have changed as the chapter closes?

2. Stephen interprets Father Arnall's sermons as a personal message, sensing that "every word" of it was intended "for him." Reread the sermons carefully. What can you identify about the language and rhetorical strategy of the sermons that would appeal so strongly to Stephen? Some things to look for in the descriptions of hell might include: the descriptions of hell's torments, the language of exile used here; the poetic and metaphorical language; and the language of the senses and the body.

3. What is the effect of the narrator aligning us with Stephen Dedalus' perspective during the sermons? How does this color our perspective toward the sermons, which seem otherwise to be presented word-for-word? How would the chapter read differently if it were aligned with the perspective of Vincent Heron, for example? Does our awareness of Stephen's idiosyncratic character affect our understanding of the communion scene at the end?

SECTION FIVE

Chapter 4

New Characters:

The Director: *at Belvedere College, asks Stephen to consider joining the priesthood*

Dan Crosby: *a tutor, who goes with Stephen's father to find out about the university for Stephen*

Dwyer, Towser, Shuley, Ennis, Connolly: *acquaintances of Stephen's; he sees them swimming near the strand*

Summary

Stephen has now dedicated his life to the service of God—each day is structured around prayer, ritual, and religious devotions. He attends mass each morning, and offers ejaculations and prayers each day for the souls in purgatory. He sees his daily life now in terms of eternity, and senses an immediate connection between his acts on earth and their repercussions in heaven. Each of his three daily chaplets is dedicated to one of the "three theological virtues," Father, Son and Holy Ghost; each day of the week is devoted toward gaining one of the seven gifts of the Holy Ghost, and toward driving out each of the seven deadly sins.

Stephen views every aspect of his life as a gift from God; the world now exists for him "as a theorem of divine power and love and universality." He tries to mortify and discipline each of his senses. He keeps his eyes to the ground, doesn't try to avoid loud or unpleasant noises, intentionally subjects himself to unpleasant smells, and is strict about his diet, making sure he does not enjoy his food. He goes to great efforts to remain physically uncomfortable, both while sleeping and awake.

He is discouraged that, despite his efforts, he continues to get angry or impatient with others for trivial reasons. However, he takes great pleasure in being able to avoid temptation, though he periodically doubts how completely he has changed his life. In confession, he sometimes has to repeat an earlier sin because he sins so infrequently now. Stephen is frustrated, because it seems that he will never be able to fully escape the sins which he had struggled to confess at the end of Chapter Three.

In the next section, Stephen is speaking with the director of Belvedere College. He has been summoned to the director's office, and, while making friendly and respectful small-talk, Stephen wonders why he has really been sent there. They begin talking about the Dominican and Franciscan orders, and of their respective styles of dress.

Stephen begins to think about his experiences with the Jesuits at school. He continues to hold them in high regard, although they sometimes seem "a little childish" in their judgments.

The director soon comes to the point, however, asking if Stephen has ever felt a vocation to join the priesthood. Stephen starts to answer "yes," but remains silent. He tells the priest that he has "sometimes thought of it." The priest tells him that only one or two boys from the college will be the sort who will be called by God, and suggests that Stephen, with his intelligence, devotion, and leadership qualities, might be one. The priest begins to talk of the power and authority a priest has, which reminds Stephen of "his own proud musings" on the subject, when he had imagined himself as a priest. The idea seems to appeal to him—he is attracted to the secret knowledge and power the priesthood could give him.

The priest tells him that his mass the next morning will be specially dedicated so that God may reveal His will to Stephen. He cautions Stephen to be certain of his decision, because it is a final one, on which the salvation of his soul may depend.

As he leaves the director's office, Stephen and the director shake hands. Stephen notes the gravity of the expression on the priest's face. Walking home, he tries to imagine himself as a priest. Remembering the "troubling odour" of Clongowes, he begins to

feel restless and confused. He begins to imagine how restless and unhappy he would be, and quickly decides that he could not become a priest, that "he would fall," and that "his destiny was to be elusive of social or religious orders."

Stephen arrives at home, where his brothers and sisters are having tea. He learns that his parents have gone to look at another home. The family is moving again, under pressure from the landlord. The children start to sing, and soon Stephen joins them. It pains him to hear the "overture of weariness" in their young voices, and he thinks sadly of the "weariness and pain" of all generations of children.

In the next section, Stephen is pacing anxiously as his father and Dan Crosby, his tutor, have gone to find out about the university for him. After an hour of waiting, he leaves for the Bull, a sandy island near the mouth of the Liffey.

While walking, he thinks of the university. He knows his mother is hostile to the idea, which Stephen takes as an indication of how their lives are drifting apart. He still feels that he has been born for some special purpose, and he senses that the university will lead to new adventures.

As he crosses the bridge on the way to the Bull, he passes a squad of Christian Brothers, walking two by two. He has a moment of shame or regret for refusing to join the priesthood, but reassures himself that their life is not for him.

He thinks of a phrase he has read, "A day of dappled seaborne clouds," and marvels at how the words seem to capture the moment so perfectly. He muses about what it is that fascinates him about words.

Having crossed the bridge, he heads toward the sea. Looking at the clouds coming in from the sea, he thinks of Europe, where they have come from. His reverie is interrupted, however, by a group of his classmates who are bathing in the sea. They call to him, and he stops briefly to chat, impatient with their immaturity, and repulsed by their adolescent nakedness. They call his name in Latinate and Greek forms, "Stephenos Dedalos" and "Stephanoumenos," which makes him think of his name as a prophecy. He understands Daedalus, the mythical artificer, as a "symbol of the artist forging anew in his workshop out of the

sluggish matter of the earth a new soaring impalpable imperishable being," and wonders if this is an indication of his calling in life. He feels excited, and knows he must dedicate his life and soul to art.

He walks away from the boys, heading down the strand, along the sea. He sees a girl alone, wading in the sea, with her skirts pinned up around her waist. She seems to him like a bird, and he takes her as a sign of his newly chosen destiny. Their eyes meet, but they do not speak. Stephen wanders off, delirious with excitement. He has lost track of time and, realizing it is late and he has wandered far out of his way, he runs back toward the land. He lays down before long, and sleeps. When he awakes, it is evening, and the new moon has risen.

Analysis

In this crucial, climactic chapter, Stephen's awareness of his artistic vision begins to crystallize. Over the course of the chapter, he frees himself from the "nets" of the church, and from his family, embracing the role of the exile figure more explicitly than before. As the chapter ends, Stephen is alone on the seashore, facing away from Ireland, toward Europe. He has literally left his father behind, who had gone to see about the university for him. And he has left the church behind, as he decides he cannot become a priest, and must instead discover his destiny on his own, apart from the trappings of religion, family, or nation. Just as, over the course of Chapter Three, Stephen had undergone an almost total religious transformation, over the course of this chapter his outlook changes greatly. There is a progression in Chapter Four from the rigid order of Stephen's religious devotion and the promise of an even more rigid order in the priesthood, to uncertainty and loss of faith, disorder and confusion, and back to a certainty in a different kind of calling, that of creative art.

Stephen's religious devotion, at the start of this chapter, has none of the passion of his conversion. Stephen's piety is rigidly structured, almost monkish—the narrator's language in this first section is prosaic, dry and businesslike, cataloging Stephen's tight and orderly schedule of religious devotion. Again, we see how what had seemed a passionate and climactic epiphany—Stephen's repentance and

religious awakening at the end of Chapter Three—seems to become, at the start of the next chapter, a dull and habitual routine.

Stephen's religious devotion has a particularly mathematical and economical character, which tends to undercut our sense of his seriousness. The weeks and even the days of his life are broken down into numbered segments. His prayers for the souls in purgatory are described as a kind of transaction with God; Stephen is anxious that he "could never know how much temporal punishment he had remitted by way of suffrage for the agonizing souls." He constantly frets that he has not been able to amass enough to make an appreciable difference. The economic metaphors are made more explicit further on, as Stephen imagines the immediate repercussions in heaven of his acts of devotion on earth:

> At times his sense of such immediate repercussion was so lively that he seemed to feel his soul in devotion pressing like fingers the keyboard of a great cash register and to see the amount of his purchase start forth immediately in heaven.

Though Stephen is certainly adamant in his dedication to the religious life, the narrator seems to be subtly parodying his piety in passages like this. When Stephen views his prayers in terms of "the amount of his purchase," imagining a "great cash register" in heaven, his religious dedication seems simplistic and reductive.

While on the one hand this portrayal of Stephen's faith seems rather ridiculous and simplistic, on the other hand, it represents a vividly imaginative kind of belief. In a manner which is typical of Stephen, his religious life colors his daily life in every aspect—he now understands his life in terms of eternity, and imagines heaven's response to his every action. His imagination is typically poetic and metaphorical in character. For example, when he recites the rosary prayers while walking down the street, he imagines the beads "transformed...into coronals of flowers of such vague unearthly texture that they seemed to him as hueless and odorless as they were nameless." His daily rituals, although certainly routine and habitualized to an extreme degree, represent for Stephen an active and vivid imaginative life.

Religion, for Stephen, serves to keep him detached from ordinary Dublin life—its effect on his imagination can be accurately compared to the effect of the *Count of Monte Cristo in* Chapter Two. Although it is imaginative, however, his devotion becomes less and less passionate. He can comprehend minute theological details, but cannot conceive of the notion of God's eternal love:

> The imagery through which the nature and kinship of the Three Persons of the Trinity were darkly shadowed forth in the books of devotion which he read...were easier of acceptance by his mind by reason of their august incomprehensibility that was the simple fact that God had loved his soul from all eternity, for ages before he had been born into the world, for ages before the world itself had existed.

It is not just God's love which Stephen finds difficult to understand or to feel:

> He had heard the names of the passions of love and hate pronounced solemnly on the stage and in the pulpit, had found them set forth solemnly in books, and had wondered why his soul was unable to harbour them for any time or to force his lips to utter their names with conviction.

Books do not connect to life for Stephen, and his faith is more intellectual than emotional. Once the lust from which he suffered has been effectively banished, his mind is left "lucid and indifferent." The same kind of indifference that had characterized Stephen's spiritual life before his conversion is used to characterize him now—the narrator suggests that in some sense maybe Stephen's life has not charged as completely as it may seem.

He is still cut off from other people, for example. There is a detached, intellectual quality to his religious faith. He looks at the world as evidence of divine power, but in a way that does not necessarily reveal any appreciation or love for the beauty in the world:

> The world for all its solid substance and complexity no longer existed for his soul save as a theorem of divine power and love and universality.

Stephen is certainly "otherworldly" in his religious devotion. It is as if his life is only a brief preparation for eternity, part of some "divine purpose" that he "dared not question." It is difficult for him to "understand why it was in any way necessary that he should continue to live."

The absurdities of his efforts to mortify his senses illustrate how his religious faith is cutting him off from the world around him. This contrasts strongly with the extremely physical language which characterized Stephen at the start of Chapter Three, and represents one way that he has changed in Chapter Four. One way he has not changed, however, is how detached he is from life around him. In Chapter Three, it was as a result of this physicality, and the nature of his sin, that he felt no sense of community with those around him. In this chapter, after the communion scene with Stephen kneeling among his classmates, we might assume that he is now on some common ground with them, and is a part of their community. Instead, however, he finds that "To merge his life in the common tide of other lives was harder for him than any fasting or prayer." Despite his efforts, he is still isolated from his peers. Religion for Stephen is an intensely private, almost solipsistic experience, and becomes only one more way that he feels alienated from those around him.

In some ways, we might suspect that Stephen's religious transformation is incomplete. But his dedication is so extreme that when the director of Belvedere asks him if he has considered joining the priesthood, we may very well assume that he will accept the offer. His devotion is already very priestlike in its rigid self-discipline, and in its effect of keeping him cut off from the flow of ordinary life. He indeed seems, as the priest suggests, an ideal candidate.

At the same time, however, many aspects of the language used to describe this scene prefigure Stephen's rejection of the offer, and ultimately of the church and religious life altogether. The priest himself is described in the language of death and stagnation:

> The priest's face was in total shadow but the waning daylight from behind him touched the deeply grooved temples and the curves of the skull.

His face, which we would associate with a living individual, is not visible in the dim light. Only his skull, which we associate with anonymity and death, can be perceived. His voice is described more than once as "grave and cordial," and the double meaning of "grave" resonates strongly. The hour of dusk suggests a fading and waning life.

When they begin talking about the styles of dress of different orders of the priesthood, and how they are often impractical and ridiculous, the extent to which a priest must remain detached from normal life is emphasized. This, of course, should appeal to Stephen, as he has seen himself as detached from normal life for some time now. But the wandering of Stephen's mind as the priest is slowly leading up to his point suggests that perhaps he is not ready for this kind of commitment:

> The names of articles of dress worn by women or of certain soft and delicate stuffs used in their making brought always to his mind a delicate and sinful perfume.... It had shocked him too when he had felt for the first time beneath his tremulous fingers the brittle texture of a woman's stocking....

It is not an encouraging sign that Stephen is thinking, with no sign of guilt or regret, of his experiences with the prostitutes while the priest is building up toward asking him to consider joining the priesthood.

Stephen's attitude toward the priest is similarly suggestive of his eventual refusal. He is respectful, but also somewhat impatient and indulgent as he waits for the priest to stop beating around the bush. This reflects his overall attitude toward the Jesuits these days. He is respectful of the order, and all they have done for him, but he is also subtly dissatisfied with them. He thinks fondly and without resentment of the way they ran the schools he has attended—he has even forgiven the pandying incident from Chapter One. However, he associates the Jesuits with a younger phase of his life, and it does not seem that he will continue among them:

> Lately some of their judgments had sounded a little childish in his ears and had made him feel a regret and pity as though he were slowly passing out of an accustomed world and were hearing its language for the last time.

He remembers an incident where a priest was condemning Victor Hugo for turning against the church, which incites an "unresting doubt" in Stephen's mind. He associates Jesuit authority with his childhood, and it is apparent that he has matured since then, and is beginning to feel superior to them in some ways.

Despite these numerous suggestions to the contrary, the idea of the priesthood does appeal to Stephen initially. He has indeed thought of it before this, and the priest speaks directly to the aspects of the priesthood that appeal most to Stephen: the privilege, power, and prestige of the office. His initial response is positive:

> A flame began to flutter again on Stephen's cheek as he heard in this proud address an echo of his own proud musings. How often he had seen himself as a priest wielding calmly and humbly the awful power of which angels and saints stood in reverence! His soul loved to muse in secret on this desire. He had seen himself, a young and silent mannered priest, entering a confession swiftly, incensing, genuflecting, accomplishing the vague acts of the priesthood which pleased him by reason of their semblance of reality and of their distance from it.

Both the priest's description and Stephen's response recall one of his earlier vices: pride. The appeal of the priesthood for Stephen involves power, secrecy, and access to privileged knowledge. He pictures himself a priest, in a highly dramatic and literary fashion. It represents for him a "secret desire," a fantasy. There is an unhealthy degree of sexual voyeurism and self-satisfied pride in his hope to "know the sins, the sinful longings and sinful thoughts and sinful acts, of others, hearing them murmured into his ears in the confessional under the shame of a darkened chapel by the lips of women and girls."

Stephen imagines taking pleasure in hearing other people's sins, and in the pride he would feel at being above and beyond such a sinful existence: "no touch of sin would linger upon the hands with which he would elevate and break the host." It is almost as if the priesthood would afford an opportunity to vent the desires he apparently is not free from, but in a "safe," sinless environment.

His reasons for being attracted to the priesthood are all self-indulgent and proud. He has no thoughts of helping others, of the benefits of his works on the world around him. The priest's description of the power and privilege, and Stephen's fantasies, all glorify the priesthood for the wrong reasons. This suggests again that Stephen is perhaps not as changed as it would seem.

Stephen's picture of a priestly life is one of isolation, which is consistent with the role of exile which has appealed to him in different forms throughout the novel. As he comes out of the director's office, this isolation from his peers is emphasized:

> Towards Findlater's church a quartet of young men were striding along with linked arms, swaying their heads and stepping to the agile melody of their leader's concertina.

Stephen stands apart, alone; we could never picture him strolling across campus in this manner. The students' "linked arms" recall the "living rail of hands" of which Stephen is a part in the communion scene at the end of Chapter Three. His aspiration to become a part of his community has been abandoned, and indeed his imaginative visualization of himself as a priest emphasizes his singularity and detachment.

In fact, it is the thought of the community of the priesthood which changes his mind. He realizes that life as a priest would cost him the individuality he has cultivated for so long:

> The chill and order of the life repelled him. He saw himself rising in the cold of the morning and filing down with the others to early mass and trying vainly to struggle with his prayers against the fainting sickness of his stomach. He saw himself sitting at dinner with the community of a college. What, then, had become of that deeprooted shyness of his which had made him loth to eat or drink under a strange roof? What had come of the pride of his spirit which had always made him conceive of himself as a being apart in every order?

Again, he imagines himself, pictures himself a priest, but this time in a more negative light. The idea of being part of a community of priests, one among many, does not appeal to Stephen's sense of pride or individuality. He remembers that his sense of a special purpose for his life had always been rooted in the keen sense that he is special, that he is unlike other people, a "being apart in every order":

> He would never swing the thurible before the tabernacle as a priest. His destiny was to be elusive of social or religious orders.... He was destined to learn his own wisdom apart from others or to learn the wisdom of others himself wandering among the snares of the world.

The commitment involved in joining the community of the priesthood threatens to stifle Stephen's individual ego. When he rejects the priesthood, he affirms the "snares of the world," and accepts the idea that to fulfill his destiny, he may have to sin in the eyes of the church:

> The snares of the world were its ways of sin. He would fall. He had not yet fallen but he would fall silently, in an instant. Not to fall was too hard, too hard....

Stephen accepts the idea that to sin is human, and that the rigid constraints of his religious faith will continue to threaten his freedom to develop.

As he returns, the disorder of the Dedalus household symbolically contrasts with the "order" of the priesthood. While earlier in the novel, the declining status of the family's wealth had caused Stephen despair and shame, he now embraces it. This represents his new perspective on his life: Stephen affirms disorder, fluidity and change over the rigidity and commitment of the priesthood. As he joins his younger brothers and sisters in song—probably the most notable example of familial love in the novel—he seems to feel more at home with them than he would ever feel in the company of priests. As this section ends, Stephen is thinking of the privileges he has had, which his younger siblings will not have. "All that had been denied them had been freely given to him, the eldest: but the quiet glow of evening showed him in their faces no sign of rancour." In a rare selfless moment, Stephen seems to appreciate the opportunities he had despite his family's decline.

In the final section of the chapter, we have what is considered by most readers to be the major climax of the novel. Stephen has gone off alone, along the seashore. Seeing a girl bathing alone, he has an intense vision of his life as an artist. However, the narrative leaves open the possibility that this climax may be somewhat ironic, and that Stephen might be under a delusion. After all, Chapter Three had ended with a spiritual climax of comparable energy—by now we are perhaps more suspicious.

Stephen's artistic awakening is spawned initially by a poetic phrase, "A day of dappled seaborne clouds," which came to mind as he walked alone. Stephen has been fascinated by language since he was a young boy, only here his enthusiasm is given a more complete expression, and more directly affects his conception of his life. He turns this phrase over and over in his mind, fascinated by the sound and rhythm of the words themselves.

His reverie is interrupted, however, as he comes across a group of his classmates bathing. Once again, Stephen's imaginative "voices," in this case the European voices "from beyond the world" of Dublin, are interrupted by literal, earthbound voices, those of the boys calling his name. This is similar to the moment when, in his religious trance, Stephen heard the voices of hell and the narrator juxtaposed those against the voices of Mr. Tate and Vincent Heron speaking in ordinary, casual voices. Here, the narrator creates a stark contrast between the world of Stephen's imagination and the reality that surrounds him. He is repulsed by the sight and sound of these boys, and sets himself apart from them:

> He stood still in deference to their calls and parried their banter with easy words. How characterless they looked: Shuley without his deep unbuttoned collar, Ennis without his scarlet belt with the snaky clasp, and Connolly with out his Norfolk coat with the flapless sidepockets! It was a pain to see them and a swordlike pain to see the signs of adolescence that made repellent their pitiable nakedness.... But he, apart from them and in silence, remembered in what dread he stood of the mystery of his own body.

There is an interesting combination of identification and distance in this passage. Stephen is still clearly trying to separate himself from the other boys his age—he stands apart, silent, and only engages with them in a superficial and detached manner. He is pained by what he has in common with them, but in this pain he recognizes a kind of common bond with his peers, a limit to his pose of detachment. The narrator shows us both how distinct Stephen is from others his age, while at the same time suggesting that his dreams and fantasies are primarily imaginative. He is perhaps not as different from other boys as he thinks.

When Stephen sees the girl bathing in the sea, he interprets every aspect of their wordless encounter in symbolic terms—she seems to him like a bird, representing Ireland, sexuality, femininity and creation all at once. The image of a bird suggests Stephen's new desire for flight from Ireland, to be free of the "nets" of religion, nation, and family. He interprets this encounter as an otherworldly visitation, a profound spiritual experience that validates and christens his new conception of himself as an artist.

When he encounters the girl, we already know that Stephen is especially ripe to interpret things symbolically. This new capacity is one manifestation of his artistic and poetic awakening, and stems directly from his meditation on language and its mysterious appeal. When the boys interrupt his thoughts about language and poetry, they call his name in pseudo-Greek and Latinate constructions. Stephen then recognizes an aspect of his name that he had not considered before—he thinks of the mythological figure of Daedalus, the great artificer, and Icarus his son, who escaped from Crete using wings which Daedalus created out of feathers and beeswax. He takes this as a kind of "prophecy," a sign that the role of creator is the special purpose he has sensed since childhood. The figure of Daedalus also suggests the escape Stephen imagines his art will be able to provide—an escape both from dull, ordinary life, and from Dublin and Ireland:

> Now, at the name of the fabulous artificer, he seemed to hear the noise of dim waves and to see a winged form flying above the waves and slowly climbing the air. What did it mean? Was it a quaint device opening a page of some medieval book of prophecies and symbols, a hawklike man flying sunward above the sea, a prophecy of the end he had been born to serve and had been following through the mists of childhood and boyhood, a symbol of the artist forging anew in his workshop out of the sluggish matter of the earth a new soaring impalpable imperishable being?

The reference to a "hawklike man flying sunward" suggests Icarus rather than Daedalus, who disregarded his father's advice and flew too close to the sun, fatally melting his wings. This suggests the amount of risk involved in Stephen's imaginative bid for freedom, and how the pride that has been his vice in the past might ultimately lead to his destruction.

Thinking about his name and the vision it inspires, Stephen immediately asks himself, "what did it mean?" He now assumes that things around him can have symbolic import, and so when he encounters the girl in the water, his immediate perception reveals a complex process of interpretation:

> A girl stood before him in midstream, alone and still, gazing out to sea. She seemed like one whom magic had changed into the likeness of a strange and beautiful seabird. Her long slender bare legs were delicate as a crane's and pure save where an emerald trail of seaweed had fashioned itself as a sign upon the flesh.

This scene, like any in the novel, is mediated by Stephen's consciousness. We observe him interpreting her as a symbol, rather than reading her as one ourselves. Stephen is transforming everything about her as he perceives it, and we are always aware that this is only a representation of how she "seemed" to him. And his interpretive process is complex and multi-leveled: she is as a seabird, and both the sea and the potential for flight suggest Stephen's turn of attention away from Ireland and toward Europe. The "emerald" trail of seaweed clearly suggests Ireland (the "emerald isle), and he interprets this immediately and without hesitation "as a sign."

This scene is richly suggestive in its symbolism in its own right, and can indeed inform and influence our interpretation of the novel and Stephen's artistic awakening. This double-leveled structure, by which we are experiencing the symbol at a remove, seeing him make a symbol out of her, allows us a distinct distance from the scene. We might feel that this is not "really" a symbol at all, but merely an example of the narrator showing us the temper of Stephen's mind at the time, which causes him to see his life in a symbolic light. We might feel that the narrator is creating another "false climax," as he has in every chapter so far, and that Stephen is really deluded in his enthusiasm and certainty. By now we are certainly suspicious of Stephen's revelations; we might not be as sure as Stephen that his name is a "prophecy."

The narrative artfully leaves all its options alive. The tone of these closing pages is genuinely triumphant, and these symbols, which Stephen recognizes, are indeed richly suggestive and multivalent in their own right, and really do offer some useful interpretive perspectives on the meaning of the novel as a whole. At the same time, the pace of this narrative has fostered in us a suspicious and subtly ironic attitude toward Stephen. We are not easily convinced, by this point in the novel, that Stephen's epiphanies are genuine. Our experience of this profound moment of significance in Stephen's life remains contingent on the developments of the next chapter. Either Stephen has had a spiritual awakening and will dedicate his life to artistic creation, and will continue to distance himself from his religion and nation in an effort to serve this end, or, like his religious awaking, this will prove to be another instructive delusion.

Study Questions

1. Describe Stephen's daily life at the start of Chapter Four.

2. Why does Stephen have trouble mortifying his sense of smell?

3. What is Stephen's opinion of the Jesuits now?

4. How does Stephen reply when the director of Belvedere asks him if he feels he may have a vocation for the priesthood?

5. What appeals to Stephen about the priesthood?

6. What repels Stephen about the priesthood?

7. Why aren't Stephen's parents at home when he gets in?

8. What phrase comes to Stephen's mind as he crosses the bridge to the Bull?

9. What symbolic import does Stephen recognize in his name?

10. How does Stephen interpret his encounter with the bathing girl along the strand?

Answers

1. Stephen's day is structured around religious devotions—he attends morning Mass each day, carries his rosary in his pocket, and prays systematically throughout the day. He says three chaplets a day for the three theological virtues, while dedicating each day toward gaining one of the seven gifts of the Holy Ghost, and toward driving out each of the seven deadly sins.

2. Stephen has trouble mortifying his sense of smell because he finds that he has little natural repugnance to odor, and it is difficult for him to find a smell unpleasant enough to disturb him. He ultimately finds that the smell of "long-standing urine" does the trick.

3. Stephen still respects the Jesuits, and is grateful for all they have done for him, but he admits that their judgments and opinions now seem "a little childish" to him. It is clear that Stephen feels that he is outgrowing a phase of his life that the Jesuits represent.

4. Stephen replies that he has "sometimes thought of it," but he remains noncommittal.

5. Stephen is attracted to the power, privilege, and secret knowledge that the priesthood would offer. He is eager to learn the theological secrets, and to hear people's secret confessions.

6. Stephen realizes that to become a priest would be to sacrifice an important degree of his individuality. The idea of being an anonymous member of a community of priests ultimately causes Stephen to reject the director's offer.

7. His younger sister tells him that they have gone to look at another house. Apparently, the family will have to move again, under pressure from the landlord.

8. Stephen thinks of the phrase "A day of dappled seaborne clouds," and is fascinated by the way it seems to capture the moment perfectly. Stephen is fascinated by the sound and rhythm of the words as much as their sense.

9. Stephen reads his name, Dedalus, as a "prophecy." Daedalus was the mythical artificer who escaped from Crete with his son Icarus, using wings built from wax and feathers. Stephen sees Daedalus as a symbol of both art and flight.

10. Stephen interprets her as a symbol, an affirmative sign of his new understanding of his destiny as an artist. She seems to him like a seabird, who represents art, sexuality, femininity, and Ireland.

Suggested Essay Topics

1. Consider the narrator's description of Stephen's daily religious devotions. What does the language used suggest about the nature of Stephen's piety? Does it foreshadow in any way his ultimate rejection of religious life?

2. Compare Stephen's artistic awakening in Chapter Four to his religious awakening in Chapter Three. How are they similar in their effects on Stephen's life, and in the language in which they are presented? In what ways are they different? What do these similarities and differences suggest about the larger themes of the novel?

3. At the end of Chapter Four, Stephen begins to read his name symbolically, as a "prophecy." Then, as he sees the girl bathing on the strand, he interprets this, too, as a "sign." Reread these scenes carefully. What do the symbolic meanings suggested here tell us about the novel as a whole? How do they add to our understanding of Stephen's character?

Chapter 5

New Characters:

Temple: *a gypsy socialist student, he is the instigator of the debate*

Lynch: *student at the university, to whom Stephen sounds off about his theory of aesthetics*

Donovan: *student whom Stephen dislikes; Stephen and Lynch see him on their walk*

Father Moran: *priest with whom Stephen thinks Emma flirts*

Dixon: *medical student at the library with Cranly*

The Captain: *a dwarfish old man, whom Stephen sees at the library*

O'Keefe: *student who riles Temple outside the library*

Goggins: *stout student outside the library*

Glynn: *young man at the library*

Summary

At the start of the final chapter, Stephen is sitting at breakfast in his parents' house. Pawn tickets for clothing are on the table next to him, indicating that the family had to sell more possessions. He asks his mother how fast the clock is, and she tells him he had better hurry. His sisters are asked to clear a spot for Stephen to wash at the sink, and his mother scrubs his neck and ears for him, remarking how dirty he is. His father shouts down to ask if Stephen has left yet, and his sister answers "yes." Stephen makes a sarcastic remark and leaves out the back.

As he is walking, he hears a mad nun yelling in the madhouse, "Jesus! O Jesus! Jesus!," which disturbs and angers Stephen. He is trying to forget about the "voices" of his parents, and religion. Walking alone, he thinks of plays and poems, and the aesthetic theories of Aristotle and Aquinas. He passes a clock that tells him it is eleven o'clock. He tries to remember the day of the week, thinks of the lectures he is scheduled to attend, and realizes that he is late for English. He thinks of that class, and begins to think about his close friend, Cranly. He composes nonsense verse idly in his head, and thinks of the etymology of the word "ivory." He thinks of his Latin studies and Roman history. He sees Trinity, which depresses him, and he looks at the statue of Thomas Moore, the national poet of Ireland. He thinks with affection of his friend Davin, the peasant student, and of Davin's nationalistic sympathies for Ireland. Stephen remembers a story Davin told him once, about encountering a woman alone at night while he was walking on the road, and being invited to her house to spend the night.

His reverie is interrupted by a flower seller, whom Stephen tells he has no money. He walks on and, when he arrives, he realizes it is too late for his French class, too. He goes in early to physics, instead. The physics hall is empty, except for the Dean of Studies, who is lighting a fire. The dean tells Stephen to pay attention, and learn the art of firestarting, one of the "useful arts." Stephen watches silently. They begin comparing different conceptions of art and beauty. Stephen quotes Aquinas, and defines beauty as "that which, when seen, pleases us." The priest asks Stephen when he plans to write his aesthetic theory, and Stephen humbly says he hopes to work up some ideas from Aristotle and Aquinas. Stephen begins to feel uncomfortable around the dean, and perceives the dean's partial attention to what he is saying. They begin to casually debate the usage of the world "funnel," which Stephen does not recognize because in Ireland it is called a "tundish." The priest is English, and Stephen thinks his interest in the new word is feigned. Stephen tries to return to his original subject, and thinks with some distress that the language they are speaking is the dean's national language, not his. Stephen becomes disheartened with their conversation, and the class begins to fill with students. The priest gives Stephen some conventional advice,

and hurries away. Stephen stands at a distance and watches him greet the students.

When the professor comes in, the students respond with "Kentish fire"—a stomping of the feet which could represent either applause or impatience. The professor calls roll, and Stephen's friend Cranly is not in class. A student named Moynihan sarcastically suggests that Cranly is at Leopardstown, a horse racing track. Stephen borrows a piece of notepaper from Moynihan, and idly begins to take notes. Moynihan whispers a ribald joke about "ellipsoidal balls," which causes Stephen to imagine the faculty of the university playing and laughing like animals. A northern Irish student, MacAlister, asks a question, and Stephen thinks about how much he hates this student.

After class, as the students file into the hall, they encounter a student named MacCann who is gathering signatures for a political petition. Cranly, who is waiting outside for Stephen, says, in Latin, that he has signed the petition "for universal peace," in support of Czar Nicholas II. He asks if Stephen is in a bad mood, and Stephen answers, "no." When Moynihan walks by, makes a sarcastic comment about MacCann, and then proceeds to sign the petition, Cranly expresses his disgust. MacCann then sees and greets Stephen, gently teasing him for being late. Students begin to gather, anticipating a "war of wits." MacCann asks Stephen to sign, and a "gipsy student" named Temple begins to talk about socialism and universal brotherhood. Stephen finally responds that he is not interested, and MacCann insults him by calling him a "minor poet." Stephen tells then "keep your icon," referring to the picture of the Czar, and begins to walk away with Temple following him. Cranly leads Temple and Stephen away.

As they talk, it is clear that Temple is annoying Cranly, who attacks him periodically, and pleads with Stephen to ignore Temple. They stop with Davin to watch handball, and Cranly becomes increasingly impatient with Temple. Though Temple appears undaunted by Cranly's insults, he soon leaves. Stephen and Cranly then see their friend Lynch, and Cranly and Lynch begin to wrestle. Stephen asks Davin if he has signed the petition, and Davin nods yes. When Stephen says he hasn't signed, Davin calls him a "born sneerer." When Davin asks why he does not study Irish, Stephen

implies that it is because Emma flirts with the teacher of the Irish course. They begin to discuss Stephen's attitude toward Irish nationalism and culture. Stephen claims to want to "fly by" the "nets" of nationality, language, and religion.

Davin walks off to join Cranly and the handball players, and Stephen and Lynch walk away. They share a cigarette, and Stephen begins to explain his aesthetic theory to Lynch, who pretends to resist, claiming to be hung-over. Stephen defines "pity" and "terror" as they relate to tragedy, defining the "dramatic" and "esthetic" emotions as "static," or arrested, "raised above desire and loathing." Stephen feels that art should not excite "kinetic emotions" like desire, but should serve a more "detached" function, calling forth an "ideal pity" or "ideal desire."

Lynch continues to listen to Stephen, although reluctantly, claiming that he doesn't care about it. Stephen continues to define beauty, using Aquinas' definition, as he did while speaking to the dean earlier. He then discusses the relation between beauty and truth, according to Plato and Aristotle. His discourse is interrupted first by a drag full of iron, then by another student, Donovan, who tells them about exam results, and the field club. As he leaves, Stephen continues to detail his concept of universal beauty, and its relation to perception, and artistic structure, with Lynch now egging him on. Stephen is concerned with what he calls the three basic forms of art: lyrical, epical and dramatic, and the inter-relationship between them. Stephen's picture of artistic creation is of the artist as a kind of God, indifferent to his creation, "paring his fingernails."

As it starts to rain, they head to the library. Lynch tells Stephen that his "beloved" (presumably Emma) is there. He stands with the group silently, glancing at her from time to time. She ignores him, and soon leaves with her friends. Stephen is first bitter and resentful, but then wonders if he has judged her harshly.

As the next section begins, Stephen is waking up at dawn. He feels a seemingly divine inspiration, and begins almost spontaneously to compose lines of verse in his head. Fearing he may lose his inspiration, he gropes around and finds a pencil and cigarette pack, and writes down the first two stanzas of a villanelle. It is clear that he is thinking of Emma as he writes, and he begins to imagine himself singing songs to her. He recalls a brief exchange with her at a dance, and imagines himself as a heretical monk. He thinks of her flirting with a priest, and tells himself that he scorns her, though he admits that this is also a "form of homage."

Having composed an entire villanelle, Stephen recalls writing a poem for her ten years before (in Chapter Two), after they rode the last tram home together. He imagines sending her the poem, and thinks of her family reading and mocking it over breakfast. He then corrects himself, and says that she is "innocent," though still a "temptress." The section ends with Stephen's villanelle:

Are you not weary of ardent ways,
Lure of the fallen seraphim?
Tell no more of enchanted days.

Your eyes have set man's heart ablaze
And you have had your will of him.
Are you not weary of ardent ways?

Above the flame the smoke of praise
Goes up from ocean rim to rim.
Tell no more of enchanted days.

Our broken cries and mournful lays
Rise in one eucharistic hymn.
Are you not weary of ardent ways?

While sacrificing hands upraise
The chalice flowing to the brim,
Tell no more of enchanted days.

And still you hold our longing gaze
With languorous look and lavish limb!
Are you not weary of ardent ways?
Tell no more of enchanted days.

In the next section, Stephen is standing on the library steps, watching birds in the sky. He is thinking about his mother, and his plans to leave the country. He thinks of a line from Yeats' play *The Countess Cathleen*, and delights in the pleasurable sound of the words. He thinks with disgust of the opening night of the national theater, where the Dublin audience booed Yeats' play.

Stephen goes inside and meets his friend Cranly, who is talking with a medical student named Dixon. A priest has gone to complain about their chatter, so they decide to leave. They encounter an old man they call "the captain," who is known for his fondness for reading Sir Walter Scott. They encounter a group of students, with Temple at the center. They are joking around, for the most part, teasing Temple. Temple tries to engage Stephen into the discussion, asking if he believes in the law of heredity, while Cranly expresses his disgust. Temple says that he admits that he is a "ballocks," but that Cranly is too, and won't admit it. Emma walks past them, and greets Cranly casually. Stephen thinks of his friend Cranly, and wanders about, on the outskirts of the group thinking to himself. His reverie is interrupted as he picks a louse off his collar—his thoughts then revert to his despair about his impoverished state.

Stephen walks back to the group just as a student named Glynn has come out. They engage in further discussion, this time around the biblical phrase "suffer little children to come unto me." Temple tries to engage the group in a theological debate, but they disregard him. He pursues this, until Cranly chases him away. Stephen tells Cranly he wants to speak with him, and they walk away together.

Cranly stops to say some parting words to the other students, and Stephen goes on ahead to wait. While waiting, he looks in the window of a hotel drawing room and thinks angrily of the "patricians" of Ireland. Stephen wonders how, with his art, he could "hit their conscience" or "cast his shadow over the imaginations of their daughters."

He is soon joined by Cranly, and as they walk off arm in arm Cranly makes an angry remark about Temple. Stephen tells Cranly that he had an "unpleasant quarrel" with his mother over religion earlier that night. Mrs. Dedalus wants Stephen to observe his Easter duty, but he refuses to. Cranly calls Stephen an "excitable man" and warns him to "go easy." Cranly ask Stephen if he believes in the Eucharist, and Stephen answers that he neither believes nor disbelieves, and does not wish to overcome his doubts. Cranly remarks that Stephen's mind is "supersaturated" with the religion he professes to disbelieve.

When Cranly asks if Stephen was "happier" when he believed, Stephen responds by saying that he was "someone else" then.

Cranly asks Stephen if he loves his mother, and Stephen says he does not understand the question. He says that he tried to love God, but is not sure if he succeeded. Cranly asks if Stephen's mother has had a "happy life," and Stephen responds, "how do I know?" Cranly asks about the Dedalus family's economic history, and learns that they were once much wealthier than now. Cranly then supposes that Mrs. Dedalus has suffered much, and encourages Stephen to try to "save her from suffering more." Cranly says that a mother's love is the one sure thing in this world, and tells Stephen that this is more important than this "ideas and ambitions."

Stephen counters by naming prominent intellectuals who placed their "ideas" before their mother's love, and Cranly calls them all pigs. Stephen suggests that Jesus too treated his mother with "scant attention in public," and Cranly replies that perhaps Jesus was "not who he pretended to be," and that he was "a conscious hypocrite." When Cranly asks if it shocked Stephen to hear him say this, Stephen admits that it did. Cranly asks him why a blasphemy would shock someone who professed not to believe, and Stephen replies that he is "not at all sure" that the Catholic religion is false. Stephen admits that part of the reason he will not take communion is because he fears that God might be real. Stephen then checks himself, saying that it is not the power of the Roman Catholic version of God that he fears, but the danger to his soul of committing false homage. When Cranly asks if he will now become a Protestant, Stephen replies dryly that he has not lost his self-respect.

They pass a servant singing in a kitchen as she sharpens knives, and they stop to listen. As they move on, Cranly asks Stephen if he considers the song she sang, "Rosie O' Grady," to be "poetry," and Stephen replies that he would have to see Rosie before he could say. He then announces his plans to go away from Ireland. Cranly suggests that the church is not driving Stephen away, and that if he leaves he leaves of his own accord. He questions Stephen on some moral issues, and Stephen responds by saying that he will not serve any church or country, but will seek the freedom to express himself apart from these bonds. He says that he is not afraid to live alone, or to have made a "great," eternal "mistake." The section ends as Cranly asks Stephen how he could live with no

friends at all. Stephen suspects that Cranly is thinking of himself, but when he asks Cranly does not answer.

The novel ends with excerpts from Stephen's journal, beginning with an entry for the night following his conversation with Cranly. He writes about following women with Lynch, discussing religion with his mother (who claims he has a "queer mind" and that he reads too much), arguing about heresy with other students, and wondering what Emma is doing and thinking. He writes of his plans to leave, and he writes about a final encounter with Emma when he told her he was leaving. They shook hands, and Stephen concludes that it was "friendly." He tells himself, however, that he is over his obsession. The journal ends as Stephen is about to depart—as he vows "to encounter for the millionth time the reality of experience and to forge in the smithy of [his] soul the uncreated conscience of [his] race."

Analysis

If the novel had ended with Chapter Four, it would have been an unambiguous climax, an affirmation of Stephen's artistic vision. Such an ending would, however, have left many important questions unanswered. How would Stephen reconcile his new vision for his life with the reality of his surroundings? After all, we might say, deciding to become an artist does not make you an artist. By including Chapter Five, Joyce makes Stephen's vision more realistic. By showing the day-to-day reality the artist will still have to face, we are given a sense of how Stephen's newly understood role will play out in his life—we can see how he attempts to live up to his new ideal. Though the tone of this chapter is harder to gauge perhaps than the ending of Chapter Four—there are many instances where we suspect that Stephen is being treated somewhat ironically by the narrator—Chapter Five represents the culmination of the main themes of the novel. In this chapter we read about Stephen's developing aesthetic or artistic theory, we see the first example of his own artistic composition, and we hear of his preparation to leave Ireland for Europe.

In Chapter Five, Stephen fully articulates and defends his conception of what it takes to be an artist, and we see him progress further toward assuming and embracing the role of solitary exile which we have seen him tending toward all along. Though this chapter consists of a good deal of dialogue—Stephen speaks with others more than in any other chapter of the novel—these conversations serve to gradually set him further and further apart from his surroundings. In them, Stephen articulates his need to be alone, free of the "nets" of family, religion, and nation. As the chapter, and the novel, ends, we have Stephen's voice all alone, addressing himself in the form of a journal, unmediated by any narrative presence. Over the course of this chapter Stephen moves closer to the solitude he deems necessary for artistic creation.

As with other chapters previously, the opening pages of Chapter Five serve as an abrupt anticlimax after the triumphant and inspired tone in which Chapter Four ended. We have already recognized that of all the potential climaxes of the novel, Stephen's artistic awakening in Chapter Four seems least prone to the narrator's irony. In Joyce's novel, the ideal of a "climax" is not the same as in more conventional fiction, where the climax is defined by the progression and culmination of a plot. In *A Portrait of the Artist as a Young Man*, all the significant "action" is internal, and therefore the climax of the novel will be in the form of a significant moment for the protagonist—a moment of "epiphany." The moment where Stephen decides he must reject his country and his religion in the name of art, when he begins to perceive his life in symbolic terms and therefore to "understand" the significance of his name, is clearly a pivotal and climactic moment in the novel—one on which our ultimate understanding of Stephen's character rests. However, this tone of triumph is sobered dramatically as Chapter Five begins.

The language with which the narrator describes Stephen at breakfast is dismal and depersonalized:

> He drained his third cup of watery tea to the dregs and set to chewing the crusts of fried bread that were scattered near him, staring into the dark pool of the jar. The yellow dripping had been scooped out like a boghole....

The way his eating is described makes it seem mechanical and numb—he "drains" the cup of tea, and "sets to chewing" the crusts of bread. The sense of images in this opening paragraph are all rather unpleasant—the "dark pool," "yellow drippings," and "boghole" are all distinctly unappetizing. We are reminded that the family is in dire economic shape by the pawning tickets on the table—Mr. Dedalus has made some of them out under false names, presumably out of shame. These first pages represent a marked drop in intensity from the previous chapter.

There is some suggestion in these opening pages that Stephen has perhaps not grown past the trappings of his surroundings at all, and that indeed he has regressed. In the first paragraph, we are told that the contents of the jar remind him of "the dark turfcoloured water of the bath in Clongowes, and we recall Stephen's younger days in the first chapter. By pulling our attention backwards in this way, after the forward-looking ending of the previous chapter, the narrator reminds us of Stephen's past, and how illusory some other "awakenings" have proven. This is further emphasized as Stephen's mother must remind him of the time, chastise him for being late for class, and even wash his face and neck for him.

His lackadaisical attitude toward his classes might seem at odds with the "new adventures" the university represented to him in the previous chapter. While Stephen's idleness and casualness at the start of the chapter might on the one hand seem like laziness or lack of energy, it also suggests a kind of patience, an attitude of inner peace and calm in the midst of his chaotic surroundings. For it is apparent that the *effects* of the previous chapter's climax are still active in Stephen's mind. There is a distinct sense, which Stephen shares, that his surroundings are holding him back, and this is the reason for the anticlimax in this chapter. It is not the case, as before, that we feel that Stephen is somehow deluded. When we saw how his religious fervor deteriorated into a dry and lifeless routine, our sense was that Stephen did not recognize this, and that the narrator was, through his choice of language, showing us that Stephen was deluded. The difference in Chapter Five is that Stephen understands that his surroundings are profoundly at odds with his conception of himself as an artist. The major substance of this chapter consists of Stephen attempting to change the squalid circumstances of his life by leaving. His daily existence then becomes a kind of challenge to his will, a test of his convictions.

That the ideals of his artistic awakening are still fully present in Stephen's mind is made clear as he leaves his house. He hears a mad nun wailing in an insane asylum, and his reaction symbolically leaves religion and family behind:

> —Jesus! O Jesus! Jesus!
> He shook the sound out of his ears by an angry toss of his head and hurried on, stumbling though the mouldering offal, his heart already bitten by an ache of loathing and bitterness. His father's whistle, his mother's mutterings, the screech of an unseen maniac were to him now so many voices offending and threatening to humble the pride of his youth. He drove their echoes even out of his heart with an execration....

He can now reduce the effects of the "voices" of family and church to simple personal threats—threats to his freedom, which he attempts to shake away with an "angry toss of the head." This chapter represents Stephen's articulation and defense of his motives and methods for seeking to distance himself from all such obligations. The calmness and quite priestlike seriousness with which he conducts himself around his friends should not be understood as a lazy kind of idleness, but rather as an attitude of patience in preparation for his life's calling. Stephen attempts to assume such a detached and disengaged posture because this is how he conceives of the proper attitude of artists in relation to their surroundings.

Stephen's artistic conversion, as he understands it, means that he must try and set himself apart form national, political, religious, and familial concerns. We have such a clear understanding of Stephen's conviction on this point because a large portion of this chapter consists of Stephen engaged in a series of significant conversations in which he defines and defends his understanding of art and its purpose, his attitude toward his country and toward political concerns, and his attitude toward his family and religion. Whereas he had been a silent observer for the greater part of the novel up to this point, now Stephen is portrayed as a relentless talker, sounding off about his developing theory of aesthetics to anyone who will listen. Four such significant conversations are the structuring principle of this chapter. We understand crucial aspects of Stephen's point of view, as well as some serious objections to it, through the conversations he has with the dean of studies, Davin, Lynch, and, most importantly, Cranly.

Stephen's conversation with the dean of studies reveals a marked change in his attitude toward authority figures once again. Priests have occupied a role of religious and practical authority for Stephen throughout the novel, though, as we observed in the last chapter, his attitude toward them had been changing of late. The subtle dissatisfaction he had felt with the Jesuits in general is now manifest in an almost condescending attitude toward the dean, who is for Stephen supposed to be a figure of academic as well as religious authority. As the dean promises to teach Stephen the art of lighting a fire, Stephen reflects to himself that the dean seems fawning and servile:

> Kneeling thus on the flagstone to kindle the fire and busied with the disposition of the wisps of paper and candelbutts he seemed more than ever a humble server making ready the place of sacrifice in an empty temple, a levite of the Lord. ...His very body had waxed old in lowly service of the Lord...and yet had remained ungraced by aught of saintly or of prelatic beauty.

Stephen now sees no value in such servitude—indeed, the theme of this chapter for him is an attempt to separate himself from all sorts of service to others. His disdain for the priest's air of servitude recalls his reaction to the "droll statue" of the national poet of Ireland on his way to class, in which he detects "sloth of the body and of the soul," and a "servile head...humbly conscious of its indignity." Stephen is now eager both to judge, and to set himself apart from, figures of authority both in the artistic and religious realms.

Stephen's attitude toward the dean during their brief discussion is one of polite impatience, almost condescension. While he sets the dean up in his mind as an example of all that is wrong with the priesthood, there is much about this man's manner in particular which irritates Stephen. When the dean invites him to learn one of the "useful" arts, this sets up Stephen's discourse about aesthetics perfectly, since his conception, as we will see, is that "usefulness" is not one of the proper purposes for art. The priest asks Stephen how he would define the "beautiful," and Stephen quotes Aquinas—"beauty is that which, when seen, pleases us." The dean encourages Stephen to pursue these questions, and to write something on them, but his responses to Stephen indicate that he is not especially interested. He is noncommittal and unconvincing in his remarks. When the dean says, "Quite so, you have certainly hit the nail on the head," or, "I see. I quite see your point," we are not at all convinced that he either understands or is interested. We can perhaps read his words of encouragement more as a somewhat perfunctory exercise of his duties as dean of the university. Stephen seems to perceive this, and eventually loses interest in the conversation. The dean does not function for Stephen here as an intellectual peer to engage and interact with in a discussion of ideas. Rather, Stephen takes this opportunity to speak about himself and his interests (an opportunity, as we will see, that he rarely passes up), and we can tell by his private responses to the dean that he is never seriously considering the dean's remarks, but rather using him as an example of the priesthood in general.

Part of Stephen's feeling of distance from the dean seems to come from the fact that the dean is English. When the dean uses the word "funnel," Stephen says that he has not heard this word before. Stephen calls this a "tundish," a word the priest claims not to have heard before. The priest concludes that "tundish" must be the Irish word for the English "funnel," and he offers a halfhearted interest in the question, claiming, "That is a most interesting word. I must look that word up. Upon my word I must." This marks a turning point in Stephen's attitude toward the priest, as he becomes less patient, and effectively stops the conversation. This apparently is a nationalistic issue for Stephen, as he reflects to himself:

—The language in which we are speaking is his before it is mine. How different are the words *home, Christ, ale, master,* on his lips and on mine! I cannot speak or write these words without unrest of spirit. His language, so familiar and so foreign, will always be for me an acquired speech. I have not made or accepted its words. My voice holds them at bay. My soul frets in the shadow of his language.

Stephen seems to be voicing his anxiety over the fact that the Irish people, as a whole, no longer speak the Irish language. The priest then would be a representative of the conquering country, England.

These quasi-nationalistic sentiments certainly seem uncharacteristic of Stephen. English, we might say, has not seemed "uncomfortable" for him before—it was the English language in fact which he found so beautiful and rhythmic at the end of Chapter Four. Rather than take this passage at face value, as representative of Stephen's true feelings toward the language question, it is more likely that he is finding reasons to dislike the priest. The funnel/tundish debate seems to bring the issue of nationality to the foreground, but Stephen had been getting impatient with the priest's noncommittal politeness before this. The issue stays on his mind, however, as we learn in his journal that he has looked up "tundish," and found it to be an English word after all. Stephen's resentment toward the priest as it is expressed in the journal seems more personally than nationally motivated: "Damn the dean of studies and his funnel! What did he come here for to teach us his own language or to learn it from us? Damn him one way or the other."

On the same day as this conflict with the dean, we see Stephen discussing this very question with his friend Davin. Davin comes from the country, in the west of Ireland, and represents Irish nationalism in the novel—he seeks both political and cultural independence for Ireland, and believes that it is people's foremost responsibility to serve their country. In the brief conversation between Stephen and Davin, we get a clear and useful exposition of Stephen's point of view on these issues, which is consistent with his intention to remain detached from all external responsibilities.

Stephen calls Davin a "tame little goose" for signing the petition, thus equating his nationalistic ideals with subservience. Stephen is especially prone to recognize and condemn subservience lately, as he implies that Davin's enthusiasm for Irish independence is on the same scale as the bowing and fawning servitude he saw in the dean. Davin, on the other hand, criticizes Stephen as a "sneerer," indicating his dissatisfaction with Stephen's pose of detachment. A "sneerer" would not consider the issues at stake carefully, but would criticize from a safe distance. In Davin's view, to be Irish is not merely hereditary or racial—it necessarily involves a responsibility to the cause of the Irish people, and a love for the Irish culture and language. He asks Stephen, "Are you Irish at all?" When Stephen offers to show him his family tree to prove it, Davin's response is, "Then be one of us." To *be* Irish means to demonstrate your affiliation through your actions. When he asks Stephen why he dropped out of a class on Irish language and culture, Stephen indicates that "one reason" is because Emma was flirting with the priest who teaches the class. His other remarks indicate, however, that his objections run much deeper—Stephen is not very interested in Irish culture, and especially Irish nationalism. Stephen expresses his view of the situation in the following exchange:

> —This race and this country and this life produced me, he said. I shall express myself as I am.
> —Try to be one of us, repeated Davin. In your heart you are an Irishman but your pride is too powerful.
> —My ancestors threw off their language and took another, Stephen said. They allowed a handful of foreigners to subject them. Do you fancy I am going to pay in my life and person debts they made? What for?

Stephen perceives the Irish as "subjects" to another power—a situation that he cannot abide. He feels that his ancestors made the mistake, and that it should not be for him, as an individual, to pay for it. Stephen accepts the political (and therefore linguistic) circumstances of his birth and, far from feeling any responsibility on this count, seeks rather to escape the constraints these circumstances impose upon the individual:

> When the soul of a man is born in this country there are nets flung at it to hold it back from flight. You talk to me of nationality, language, religion. I shall try to fly by those nets.

We can read Davin's response to this proclamation—"Too deep for me, Stevie"—in at least two ways: either as a "serious" expression of bafflement (which would fit into Stephen's sentimental picture of him as a simple peasant), or as a critique of Stephen's extreme pose of detachment. Perhaps Davin is saying that to be "deep," in this case, is not necessarily good, if it causes one to avoid all immediate responsibilities.

Whereas Davin challenges Stephen, and provides a serious foil to his point of view, Stephen apparently finds a much more receptive audience in Lynch, whom he speaks with extensively just after his conversation with Davin. Though Lynch seems to be a more receptive audience, he is actually only a more appealing version of the dean. He playfully resists Stephen's "lecture," claiming that he has a hangover, and never seems particularly interested in the question of aesthetic value which Stephen is so fascinated by. His sarcastic commentary is his version of the dean's polite pretensions of being interested. There is the sense that no one will argue extensively with Stephen on these points because aesthetic questions are not as important to anyone else as to him.

Stephen's conversation with Lynch is more like a lecture, or a monologue, than a dialogue in earnest. Stephen is espousing his aesthetic theory, while Lynch serves as the opportunity for Stephen to talk. His contributions to the conversation are in the form of crude jokes, mock protestations, and halfhearted objections. Their long conversations, while they walk through Dublin on the way to the library, represents Stephen's intellectual development up to this point—he gives a detailed exposition of his aesthetic theory, which is impressive in its scope and sophistication.

Stephen is seeking both to define beauty and the concept of the beautiful, and to define the proper place of the artist in relation to his or her creation. Stephen bases his definition of beauty mostly on the work of Aristotle and Aquinas. He describes it as a "static" emotion—the beautiful does not evoke the "kinetic" emotions of desire or loathing, but exists outside of this realm in a state of purity. Stephen's view emphasizes the structure, wholeness, and harmony of a piece of art, and asserts that we can in fact define the "necessary qualities of beauty" despite the fact that different people in different cultures perceive and appreciate different qualities as beautiful:

> Though the same object may not seem beautiful to all people,
> all people who admire a beautiful object find in it certain
> relations which satisfy and coincide with the stages them-
> selves of all esthetic apprehension.

Stephen identifies three essential forms of art: the lyrical, epical, and dramatic. Stephen values the dramatic most highly, in which the author is most removed from the work of art, when the "personality of the artist...finally refines itself out of existence." Stephen's ideal image of the artist is:

> Like the God of the creation, [who] remains within or behind or beyond or above his handiwork, invisible, refined out of existence, indifferent, paring his fingernails.

This passage is often cited as Joyce's own credo of artistic creation, although, paradoxically, this would be used to warn us against identifying Joyce with his fictional self, Stephen Dedalus, too completely. Here we see how Stephen can justify his rejection of national and political concerns in favor of his pose of detachment. In his conception, the duty of the artist is first to the unity and beauty of the work of art itself—the less the personality (and therefore the political or religious agenda) of the artist comes into play, the better.

The seriousness with which Stephen's sophisticated system of aesthetics is presented to undercut significantly, however, by Lynch's persistently crude and sarcastic humor, and his only partial engagement with Stephen's monologue. Stephen seems to like Lynch, however, perhaps because he will not challenge Stephen's assertions the way Davin or Cranly will. As soon as their conversation begins, Stephen recognizes with pleasure evidence of Lynch's "culture":

> —Damn your yellow insolence, answered Lynch.
> This second proof of Lynch's culture made Stephen smile again.
> —It was a great day for European culture, he said, when you made up your mind to swear in yellow.

Apparently Lynch is more cultured than Davin, which encourages Stephen that he will be a better (less hostile) audience, although Stephen's evidence for considering him cultured amounts to nothing more than the fact that he curses in a literary way.

Earlier, Stephen had been offended by the sound of Cranly's accent, associating it with all that is ugly and unpleasant about Dublin:

Cranly's speech, unlike that of Davin, had neither rare phrases
of Elizabethan English nor quaintly turned versions of Irish
idioms. Its drawl was an echo of the quays of Dublin given
back by a bleak decaying seaport, its energy an echo of the
sacred eloquence of Dublin given back flatly by a Wicklow
pulpit.

Surely Davin's speech, though "quaint," is not "cultured," and
neither is Cranly's. However, from what we can tell, Lynch's "culture"
amounts to a habitual repetition of stock literary phrases, in order
to curse. Lynch's appeal is as artificial as Cranly's offense. In neither
case is Stephen interested in the substance of the person, but in
how good they sound. After Stephen remarks about how fond he is
of Lynch "cursing in yellow," almost every remark out of Lynch's
mouth involves some variation on "yellow." Stephen exercises a
certain amount of control over Lynch, and seems to have his respect. But the overall sense is that this is still something of a joke
to Lynch; he still seems like little more than Stephen's "yes man."
When Stephen finishes a long tirade, and Lynch does not reply right
away, he imagines "that his words had called up around them a
thought enchanted silence." The narrator is clear to phrase this as
Stephen's perception of the scene; we may suspect, instead, that
Lynch merely has not been paying attention.

   In his conversation with Cranly, which marks the end of the
narrative proper, Stephen finds a much more challenging audience.
There is the distinct sense that Stephen values Cranly as a friend
whose opinion is important. In their dialogue, there is none of the
condescension which characterized Stephen's attitude toward
Davin, Lynch, and even the dean of studies. Cranly is not afraid to
be directly critical of Stephen's ideas and actions, and he raises
significant and considerable objections to Stephen's plan to forsake
his country and family in favor of art. Stephen recognizes a certain
connection between the two of them early in their conversation:

   Their minds, lately estranged, seemed suddenly to have been
   drawn closer together, one to the other.

Cranly is perhaps the first person in the novel who Stephen seems
to engage with on equal terms—earlier in the novel he had been
intimidated by his peers and authority figures, and later in the novel

he generally feels superior to both his peers and authority figures.

Cranly raises humanistic objections to Stephen's plan, trying to show him how his rejection of church and family will cut him off from those close to him. For Cranly, it is not a matter of rejecting "religion" or "family" or "nation" in the abstract—he reminds Stephen of the real people who will be hurt by his actions. Cranly tries to turn Stephen's attention away from the abstract principle (which Stephen expresses by quoting Lucifer, "I will not serve") and toward a more practical and human level. Stephen does not view his quarrel with his mother in terms of *her* feelings—from his point of view, she is asking him to observe a false homage, a move which his integrity of soul cannot abide. Cranly urges him to consider how much she has suffered in her life, and how Stephen, by compromising and observing his Easter duty, can reduce her suffering a little. When Cranly asks him, however, if he loves his mother, Stephen claims not to understand the question. Just as Stephen tried and failed to love God, he has not been able to feel any meaningful connection with any people in his life, family or otherwise. His one-sided obsession with Emma can hardly be called "love," and his relationship with his family is, by now, as distant and detached as can be. When Cranly asks Stephen if his mother has had "a happy life," Stephen responds honestly "How do I know?" It is clear that her feelings do not come into play in his decision not to observe Easter—it is a personal matter, that has to do in his mind with his rejection of the Catholic church. Cranly's sentimental language of human compassion provides a stark contrast to Stephen's self-centered ethic of isolation and individualism:

—Whatever else is unsure in this stinking dunghill of a world a mother's love is not. Your mother brings you into the world, carries your first in her body. What do we know about what she feels? But whatever she feels, it, at least, must be real. It must be. What are our ideas and ambitions? Play. Ideas! Why, that bloody bleating goat Temple has ideas. MacCann has ideas too. Every Jackass going the roads thinks he has ideas.

Cranly tries to appeal to Stephen's (or the reader's) sentimentality. He attempts to deflate Stephen's emphasis on the unassailable virtue of an individual pursuing his destiny outside of all society by claiming that this is not so unique, that everyone thinks his or her ideas are most important. Stephen, however, appears unaffected, and quickly moves the discussion away from himself and to the subject of other famous intellectuals in history who have offended their mothers. Cranly, however, offers a perceptive critique of Stephen's assumed pose of detachment, one which many readers will take to heart.

Cranly also challenges Stephen on the more abstract, theological and philosophical bases for his rejection of Catholicism. When Stephen assumes his pose of detachment, relishing the role of religious rebel by saying he "neither believe(s) nor disbelieve(s)," and "do(es) not want to overcome" his doubts, Cranly points out that Stephen's mind is "supersaturated" with the tenents of Catholicism. Stephen cannot set himself fully outside the structure of the church, because his pose of detachment is compromised by his long history in the church. His disbelief then is necessarily rebellious, and not disinterested and detached, since he very recently did believe. While Stephen claims that he "was someone else then," there are many indications that he is perhaps not so changed from the days when he was a believer. His conception of himself and his "mission" as an artist uses the language of the priesthood. He admits that his intellectual interests make his mind a "cloister," and cut him off from the outside world just as much as the priesthood would have.

The hold the Catholic church still has upon his mind, despite his rejection of its tenets, is made clear as Stephen admits that he is not "sure" that the religion is "false," and this is part of the reason he refuses to take communion falsely. Stephen admits that he still has a certain fear of blasphemy, although he quickly checks himself and says, "I fear more than that the chemical action which would be set up in my soul by a false homage to a symbol behind which are massed twenty centuries of authority and veneration," asserting his devotion to a personal ethic which would be morally superior to the church.

Stephen's "supersaturation" with Catholicism, despite his apparent rejection of it, is demonstrated by his reaction to Cranly's blasphemy. When Cranly suggests that Jesus was "a conscious hypocrite," and "not what he pretended to be," Stephen admits that he was "somewhat" shocked to hear Cranly say this. When Cranly asks if this is why he will not take communion, because he feels and fears that God might indeed be real, Stephen admits that this is true. It seems that Cranly is really affecting Stephen here. He seems to puncture Stephen's pose of indifference and nonchalant rebellion, showing that Stephen is still profoundly affected by the religion he claims to reject. However, Stephen's tone is difficult to gauge here. He quickly checks himself, claiming "I fear many things: dogs, horses, firearms, the sea, thunderstorms, machinery, the country road at night." He tries to lump his lingering fear of God in with other "irrational" fears.

When Stephen announces his plans to leave Ireland, Cranly is quick to point out that the church is not driving Stephen away, but that he is leaving of his own accord. When Stephen says that he "has to" go, Cranly replies, "You need not look upon yourself as driven away if you do not wish to go or as a heretic or an outlaw." Cranly is saying that Stephen is assuming this role of exile himself, that he seems to *want* to be a heretic or outlaw. This, as we know, is largely true. Stephen's conception of the artist is that he must live free of all familial, patriotic and religious obligations, and he now sees Europe as the place where this is possible. Near the end of their conversation, Stephen repeats his credo again:

> I will not serve that in which I no longer believe whether it call itself my home, my fatherland or my church: and I will try to express myself in some mode of life or art as freely as I can and as wholly as I can, using for my defense the only arms I allow myself to use—silence, exile, and cunning.

Stephen's emphasis is all on himself—he detaches himself from any obligation by dismissing his family, religion, and country as something which might "call itself" home, fatherland, or church. Stephen sees himself not necessarily as "driven away," although it is clearly necessary, for him to fulfill his vision of art, to remove himself from the circumstance, the "nets," of his birth. Cranly has pointed out, throughout their discussion, the ways this is selfish and insensitive. When he suggests that Stephen, by doing so, will alienate himself from others permanently, that he will "have not even one friend," Stephen appears unaffected. As we know, he has been alone his whole life.

Although Cranly seems to raise some serious objections, and Stephen seems to respect his point of view profoundly, we can see from his first journal entry that he has not taken Cranly's remarks to heart. Stephen's account of the situation is superficial:

> Long talk with Cranly on the subject of my revolt. He had his grand manner on. I supple and suave. Attacked me on the score of love for one's mother.

Stephen describes it as if they both had been play-acting, rather than talking about issues of real consequence in both of their lives. He is more interested in Cranly's "grand manner," and proud of his own appearance of being "supple and sauve," than any of the issues their discussion raised. Cranly's passionate appeal in favor of Mrs. Dedalus' suffering, and her love for her son, is reduced to a depersonalized move in a formal debate: "attacked me on the score of love for one's mother." Stephen shows no evidence that this conversation, which voices many reasonable and serious objections to Stephen's plan of "revolt," has had any affect on him whatsoever. It is as if his mind has been made up throughout the chapter, and it shows no tendency to change now.

Stephen in his journals appears superficial and affected. He is not afraid to be alone, and has by now embraced the role of exile fully. His brief and unemotional account of his conversation with Cranly shows how his perception is limited, and we may indeed wonder what kind of artist he will be if he has no conception of human affection or connection. His act of creation, the centerpiece of Chapter Five, bears this out. He wakes up, and almost spontaneously composes a villanelle. We have already seen him in the role of art critic, or aesthetic theorist. This is the first evidence of Stephen as artist in the novel.

Stephen's artistic inspiration is presented in religious or spiritual terms—his mind is portrayed as "pregnancy" with inspiration that came from a mysterious, divine source:

> In the virgin womb of the imagination the word was made flesh. Gabriel the seraph had come to the virgin's chamber.

He imagines himself like the Virgin Mary, and while he continues to compose the poem in his head he imagines "smoke, incense ascending from the altar of the world." As Cranly will suggest, Stephen's mind is indeed still "supersaturated" with religion, and this language suggests that in some ways his new life may not be so radically transformed from his former life. He imagines himself "a priest of eternal imagination, transmuting the daily bread of experience into the radiant body of everlasting life"—his act of creation seems to give him the same kind of power he dreamed he would have as a priest.

The "subject" of his poem is presumably Emma, although the way he imagines her while he is composing suggests how much their "relationship" exists only in his mind. As with the poem he composed for her ten years earlier, the villanelle is highly abstract, and seems to be "about" or "for" her in only the most indirect way. In some ways, his composition is quite impressive. Stephen shows a definite sensitivity to the sounds of the words, and a villanelle is a rigid and strict form—using only two rhymes, repeating the lines in a regular pattern for five three-line stanzas and a quatrain. The villanelle requires discipline, skill, and control, and gains its effects more from the formal interplay of sound and repetition than it does from emotion or passion. Therefore, Stephen's first poem is abstract, symbolic, and clearly removed from anything in his immediate life. Just as his first attempt, ten years earlier, had failed by being too far removed from the situation which had inspired it, this poem, too, is emotionally flat and detached from life. Stephen, it appears, has little conception of human love or emotion, and his art serves the purpose of removing him from daily life into the realm of fantasy and escape, sound without sense. While his poem is a somewhat impressive technical and formal achievement, we may wonder if Stephen's rigid code of individualism will cause him to suffer as an artist.

In the journal entries at the end of the novel, we have Stephen's voice directly, without the potentially ironic narrator. Over the course of the chapter we have seen him gradually become more and more alone, and this is emphasized by the univocal final pages, where Stephen is essentially "talking to himself." His tone is somewhat dramatic, and it is clear that the defense mechanisms and affectations we recognized in his interactions with his peers tend to carry over into the journals, too. However, there is a definite eagerness in the passages where he anticipates his flight to Europe.

At the end of the novel, we see the young man, whom we have followed since early childhood, now an "artist," eager to leave his dreary homeland behind in favor of life, art and experience:

> *26 April:* Mother is putting my new secondhand clothes in order. She prays now, she says, that I may learn in my own life and away from home and friends what the heart is and what it feels. Amen. So be it. Welcome, O life! I go to encounter for the millionth time the reality of experience and to forge in the smithy of my soul the uncreated conscience of my race.
> *27 April:* Old father, old artificer, stand me now and ever in good stead.

The novel in Stephen's voice, seems to end on an optimistic and forward-looking note. Most of the novel has been about rejection—Stephen has had to reject the "nets" which Dublin and Catholicism have laid upon him at birth. But his attitude now is of expectation and anticipation. Our sense is that "experience" and "life" lies elsewhere, in Europe, and that his art will feed on these. Although the narrator has been puncturing his "epiphanies" throughout, here we just have Stephen's voice in what seems to be an unambiguous affirmation. But the narration's ironies, and in particular Cranly's objections, have not been forgotten by this point, giving us a complicated and multifaceted picture of the artist. We can see many of Stephen's shortcomings, but we can also recognize in him a definite skill and ambition. We may feel, as the novel ends, that he will go off and succeed in Europe, experiencing life and creating life. Or, we may feel that this is the common delusion of youth, that, as Cranly puts it, "everyone has ideas," and we have no reason to believe that Stephen Dedalus is special. If we are willing to look outside of the text, we will see that in Joyce's next novel, *Ulysses*, Stephen Dedalus is back in Dublin—he has returned for his mother's funeral and ended up staying in town for months. In light of this later novel, the ending of *A Portrait of the Artist as a Young Man* will perhaps seem to be "punctured" much as the climaxes of the individual chapters were. The symbolism he recognizes in his name suggests both the need for flight or escape, as well as the potential hazards—Icarus, Daedalus' son, flew too high and his wings were melted by the sun. The ending of the novel is suggestively ambiguous—we may see Stephen in either, or indeed both, of these ways.

Study Questions

1. Describe Stephen's attitude toward school at the start of Chapter Five.

2. What does Davin call Stephen?

3. What is the "useful art" the dean of studies promises to teach Stephen?

4. What are the two primary influences on Stephen's artistic theory?

5. What is Davin's objection to Stephen's "revolt" against religion, family, and nation?

6. What characteristic of Lynch's speech does Stephen identify with "culture"?

7. What, according to Stephen, are the three basic forms of art?

8. What kind of poem does Stephen compose in the middle of Chapter Five?

9. Describe the attitude which the other students take toward Temple.

10. When Lynch asks Stephen if he loves his mother, what does Stephen say?

Answers

1. Stephen has a casual, even lackadaisical attitude toward his schoolwork at the start of Chapter Five. He is late for lecture, and has to borrow a scrap of notepaper from Moynihan.

2. Davin calls Stephen "Stevie."

3. The dean of studies promises to teach Stephen the "useful art" of starting a fire in a fireplace.

4. Stephen's artistic theory is based heavily on the work of Aristotle and Aquinas.

5. Davin feels that an individual's primary responsibility is to his or her country, and feels that Stephen is betraying Ireland in favor of abstract, selfish aims—a view with which Stephen does not disagree.

6. Stephen recognizes Lynch's use of "yellow" as an expletive to be an example of his "culture."

7. Stephen recognizes the three basic forms of art as the lyrical, the epical, and the tragic. The tragic is the most important, since it is when the artist is able to remove himself or herself from the creation as completely as possible.

8. Stephen composes a villanelle, a strict form which consists of only two rhymes ("ways" and "rim"), five three-line stanzas, a final quatrain, and a pattern of repetition.

9. The other students tease Temple constantly, and don't take his ideas seriously.

10. Stephen replies that he does not understand the question.

Suggested Essay Topics

1. In Chapter Five, we are given a detailed exposition of Stephen's theory of aesthetics, as well as the text of his first poem since his artistic transformation. Discuss the villanelle, using the terms of Stephen's theory as he describes it to Lynch. What can this theory tell us about the poem? How does this relate to the thematic issues in this chapter?

2. Cranly suggests that, despite his claims of rejecting the Catholic church and its faith, Stephen's mind continues to be "supersaturated" with Catholicism. Discuss how this view might be used to illuminate his character in this chapter. Aspects you may want to examine include: how the narrator describes Stephen, how he describes himself, how his inspiration and act of artistic creation is described.

3. After the entire novel has been narrated through Stephen's consciousness by a third-person narrator, the novel ends with some excerpts from Stephen's journal, as he makes final preparations to leave for Europe. How does the recession of the narrative presence affect our understanding of the ending of the novel? What are some of the effects of Joyce ending the novel this way?

Sample Analytical Paper Topics

Topic #1

Examine Stephen's relationship to Catholicism as it develops throughout the novel. Use this as a way to comment on his attitude to authority more generally.

Outline

I. Thesis Statement: *Stephen's developing ethic of individualism requires him to reject the authority of the Catholic church. We can measure the progress of his artistic and individual development in part by an examination of the changes in his attitude to the priests in the novel.*

II. When he was a child, the Jesuit priests at Clongowes represented absolute authority for Stephen.

   A. His general attitude toward the priests.

   B. The pandying incident with Father Dolan, and the "resolution" of this conflict by Father Conmee.

III. His religious awakening at the retreat.

   A. The priest's voice speaks "directly to his soul," evidence of the authority Stephen grants him.

IV. His changing attitude toward the Jesuits as he gets older.

   A. Chapter Four: the director's offer; Stephen's attraction to and rejection of the priesthood.

V.   Stephen's attitude toward Catholicism as the novel ends.

   A.   His conversation with the dean of studies.

   B.   His conversation with Cranly.

Topic #2

Examine the novel's various "climaxes." In what ways does the narrator tend to treat Stephen's triumphs ironically, suggesting that he is perhaps deluded?

Outline

I.   Thesis Statement: *The narrative works according to a pattern whereby the climactic ending of each chapter is significantly deflated by the down-to-earth, routine and habitual tone of the next chapter's opening section.*

II.   Stephen's triumph at the end of Chapter One.

   A.   The plain tone of the first paragraphs of Chapter Two.

   B.   His father telling Father Conmee's version of the story at dinner.

III.   The excitement of Stephen's transgression with the prostitute at the end of Chapter Two.

   A.   How this becomes a seemingly empty and dull routine in Chapter Three.

IV.   The fervor of Stephen's confession and religious conversion at the end of Chapter Three.

   A.   How this seems passionless and routine in Chapter Four.

V.   The "climax" of the novel—Stephen's artistic conversion at the end of Chapter Four.

   A.   The narrative at the start of Chapter Five seems to suggest routine and drudgery.

   B.   This time, Stephen recognizes this, and understands that his surroundings are to blame for stifling his artistic potential (the "climax" itself is not deflated—its "puncture" has thematic significance).

VI. The eagerness and optimism of Stephen's language in the journals at the end.

    A. Is this positive tone compromised at all by this pattern of deflation in the rest of the narrative?

Topic #3

Trace the themes of exile and detachment as they develop throughout the novel.

Outline

I. Thesis Statement: *Stephen is portrayed as lonely and aloof throughout the novel, but as the novel progresses, he begins gradually to accept and embrace the role of exile until, by the end, he decides that he must leave the country and live alone in order to be happy.*

II. Stephen's "uncomfortable" loneliness at Clongowes.

    A. He feels apart from the other students, and is intimidated and uncomfortable about this.

III. In Chapter Two, his imagination (fueled by literature) causes him to detach himself from ordinary life.

    A. How this "detachment" is somewhat necessary, since the family has moved, he is no longer at school, and has no friends.

    B. How Stephen's literary imaginings suggest that he is beginning to romanticize the role of exile.

IV. After Stephen's religious conversion, his religious zeal serves to remove him from normal life.

    A. He imagines himself as a priest, separate and aloof.

V. When he has his artistic awakening at the end of Chapter Four, he decides that his pose of detachment and exile is essential toward being an artist.

    A. This pose will characterize him throughout Chapter Five.

    B. He expresses this explicitly as a personal credo of art in his conversations with Cranly and Davin.

C. His journal characterizes this, showing Stephen's voice
alone, with him looking toward Europe and his self-
imposed exile.

SECTION EIGHT

Bibliography

Blades, John. *A Portrait of the Artist as a Young Man*. Penguin Critical Studies. London: Penguin Books, 1991.

Ellmann, Richard. *James Joyce*. Second Ed. New York: Oxford U.P., 1982.

Joyce, James. *A Portrait of the Artist as a Young Man: Text, Criticism, and Notes*. Ed. Chester G. Anderson. Viking Critical Library. New York: Penguin Books, 1968.

Schutte, William M. ed. *Twentieth Century Interpretations of A Portrait of the Artist as a Young Man*. Englewood Cliffs, NJ: Prentice-Hall, 1968.

Seed, David. *James Joyce's A Portrait of the Artist as a Young Man*. New York: St. Martin's Press, 1992.

REA's **Problem Solvers**

The "PROBLEM SOLVERS" are comprehensive supplemental text-books designed to save time in finding solutions to problems. Each "PROBLEM SOLVER" is the first of its kind ever produced in its field. It is the product of a massive effort to illustrate almost any imaginable problem in exceptional depth, detail, and clarity. Each problem is worked out in detail with a step-by-step solution, and the problems are arranged in order of complexity from elementary to advanced. Each book is fully indexed for locating problems rapidly.

ACCOUNTING
ADVANCED CALCULUS
ALGEBRA & TRIGONOMETRY
AUTOMATIC CONTROL
    SYSTEMS/ROBOTICS
BIOLOGY
BUSINESS, ACCOUNTING, & FINANCE
CALCULUS
CHEMISTRY
COMPLEX VARIABLES
COMPUTER SCIENCE
DIFFERENTIAL EQUATIONS
ECONOMICS
ELECTRICAL MACHINES
ELECTRIC CIRCUITS
ELECTROMAGNETICS
ELECTRONIC COMMUNICATIONS
ELECTRONICS
FINITE & DISCRETE MATH
FLUID MECHANICS/DYNAMICS
GENETICS
GEOMETRY

HEAT TRANSFER
LINEAR ALGEBRA
MACHINE DESIGN
MATHEMATICS for ENGINEERS
MECHANICS
NUMERICAL ANALYSIS
OPERATIONS RESEARCH
OPTICS
ORGANIC CHEMISTRY
PHYSICAL CHEMISTRY
PHYSICS
PRE-CALCULUS
PROBABILITY
PSYCHOLOGY
STATISTICS
STRENGTH OF MATERIALS &
    MECHANICS OF SOLIDS
TECHNICAL DESIGN GRAPHICS
THERMODYNAMICS
TOPOLOGY
TRANSPORT PHENOMENA
VECTOR ANALYSIS

If you would like more information about any of these books,
complete the coupon below and return it to us or visit your local bookstore.

RESEARCH & EDUCATION ASSOCIATION
61 Ethel Road W. • Piscataway, New Jersey 08854
Phone: (908) 819-8880

Please send me more information about your Problem Solver Books

Name _____

Address _____

City _____ State _____ Zip _____

REA's **VERBAL BUILDER**

for Admission & Standardized Tests

Specifically designed to prepare you for all tests requiring verbal ability, including

GRE • GMAT • SAT • CLAST
LSAT • ACT • MCAT • NTE
PPST • PSAT • CBEST

REA Research & Education Association

Available at your local bookstore or order directly from us by sending in coupon below.

THE BEST TEST PREPARATION FOR THE

AP
ADVANCED
PLACEMENT
EXAMINATION

ENGLISH
Literature & Composition

by Pauline Beard, Ph.D. • Robert Liftig, Ed.D. • James Molek, Ph.D. •
James Maloney, M.A. • Joanne Miller, M.A. • Peter Trenouth, M.A. • Mattie Williams, M.A.

6 Full-Length Exams
➤ Every question based on the current exams
➤ The ONLY test preparation book with detailed explanations to every question
➤ Far more comprehensive than any other test preparation book

**Includes a COMPREHENSIVE AP COURSE REVIEW,
emphasizing all areas of literature & composition found on the exam**

REA *Research & Education Association*